CONTENTS

HUMAN RESOURCE PLANNING

	Preface	5
	Learning Profile	7
07-1	What Is Human Resource Planning?	9
07-2	Planning the Workforce	23
07-3	Job Analysis and Workforce Profiling	33
07-4	Redundancy	47
07-5	Outplacement, Redeployment and Resettlement Strategies	55
07-6	Recruitment and Selection Techniques	65
07-7	Rewards	91
	Appendices	
1	Commentary on Activities	117
2	Useful Resources	124
	Index	127

THE UNIVERSAL MANAGER SERIES

Books

01   Risk Management
02   Delivering Successful Projects
03   Planning and Controlling Projects
04   The Learning Organization
05   Managing for Knowledge
06   Obtaining and Retaining Customers
07   Human Resource Planning
08   Business Planning
09   Financial Performance
10   Managing Quality
11   Business Relationships
12   Managing for High Performance
13   Managing Harmoniously
14   21st Century Communication
15   Managing for Sustainability
16   Managing Health and Safety

Computer-based Resources

Management Assignments (CD-ROM)
Personal Development Planning Toolkit
        (at www.universal-manager.com)

PREFACE

If, as so many business leaders claim, 'people are the most important resource for any organization' why do so few organizations devote the same energy to Human Resource Planning as they do to the planning and control of financial and physical assets? The answer may lie partly in the underdevelopment of this area of management science but, as this dossier proves, there is no shortage of tools and techniques to support effective Human Resource Planning.

In this, the seventh dossier of *The Universal Manager Series* we focus on the capacity side of people planning — ensuring that the organization has the right number of the right people in the right places doing the right job. We look at the great changes in HR management which have been brought about by greater empowerment of employees, increased responsibility for line managers, enhanced flexibility in working patterns and practices, and advances in Information and Communications Technology.

Human Resource Planning will provide a useful resource for the HR or personnel specialist looking for a survey of current best practice in the field, and some pointers on likely future developments. The dossier will be particularly helpful for the non-specialist, e.g. the line manager who needs support with planning the structure, content and organization of a department or team.

5

6

DOSSIER
07

HUMAN RESOURCE
PLANNING

ACKNOWLEDGEMENTS

This publication was developed by Scitech Educational in partnership with Institute of Leadership & Management.

Project management:	Diana Thomas (Institute of Leadership & Management)
	Don McLeod (Scitech Educational)
Series editor:	Darren O'Conor
Author:	Peter Gallagher

Dossier 07: Human Resource Planning

A Scitech Educational publication

ISBN 0 948672 97 8

Published by:
Scitech Educational Ltd
Kent Innovation Centre
Millennium Way
Thanet Reach Business Park
Broadstairs
Kent CT10 2QQ
Tel: +44 (0)1843 609300
Fax: +44 (0)1843 609301
Web site: www.universal-manager.com
          www.scitech-ed.com
Email: info@scitech-ed.com

LEARNING PROFILE

Topics included in this dossier are listed below. Use them to make a quick judgement about the level of your current knowledge and understanding, and to highlight the sections of the dossier which will be most useful to you.

KEY Low	You have never or not recently studied this topic, nor recently applied the concepts at work.
Mid	You have a broad understanding of the concepts or some experience of working with them, but are not confident about your current level of knowledge.
High	You are familiar with the concepts and their theoretical underpinning. You could confidently apply the concepts in any work context.

	Low	*Mid*	*High*
(1) What Is Human Resource Planning?			
☞ Flexible models for categorizing human resources	❑	❑	❑
☞ Integrating HR planning and management into strategic and operational processes	❑	❑	❑
☞ The feedback loop through corporate, team and individual needs	❑	❑	❑
☞ The benefits of HR planning and factors which prevent organizations from applying it	❑	❑	❑
☞ Trends in sharing and outsourcing HR services	❑	❑	❑
(2) Planning the Workforce			
☞ Three essential steps in HR planning: assessing demand, forecasting supply, identifying the gap	❑	❑	❑
☞ Techniques for assessing demand, including: time series analysis; work study; productivity trends and managerial judgement	❑	❑	❑
☞ Techniques for forecasting supply, including analysis of wastage, stability and internal promotion	❑	❑	❑
☞ Sources to support analysis of the external supply of labour	❑	❑	❑
(3) Job Analysis and Workforce Profiling			
☞ The principles of effective job analysis	❑	❑	❑
☞ Job analysis methods including questionnaires and interviews (critical incident, repertory grid, hierarchical task analysis)	❑	❑	❑
☞ Trends in the use and design of job descriptions and person specifications	❑	❑	❑
☞ The use of job families to support workforce profiling, career planning and reward structures	❑	❑	❑
(4) Redundancy			
☞ The legal definition of redundancy and why it matters	❑	❑	❑
☞ Strategies for minimizing and for managing redundancies, including flexible working practices, early retirement, voluntary and targeted schemes	❑	❑	❑

(5) Outplacement, Redeployment and Resettlement Strategies
- ☞ Outplacement services and practices including the 'resource centre' approach ❑ ❑ ❑
- ☞ The benefits of effective redeployment ❑ ❑ ❑
- ☞ How HR specialists and/or line managers can support redeployment ❑ ❑ ❑
- ☞ The ethics of resettlement support for redundant employees ❑ ❑ ❑

(6) Recruitment and Selection Techniques
- ☞ CIPD guidance on effective recruitment and selection ❑ ❑ ❑
- ☞ Recruitment methods and media ❑ ❑ ❑
- ☞ Online recruitment: recent trends in usage and response rates and the likely impact of this method on future recruitment practices ❑ ❑ ❑
- ☞ The relative validity, predictive capacity and reliability of key selection techniques including interviews, ability and aptitude testing, biodata analysis, assessment centres ❑ ❑ ❑
- ☞ Competence-based recruitment and selection ❑ ❑ ❑

(7) Rewards
- ☞ The contribution of reward systems to HR strategy, and therefore overall business strategy ❑ ❑ ❑
- ☞ The main building blocks of a financial reward system: basic pay; contingent pay; allowances; benefits ❑ ❑ ❑
- ☞ Recent trends in the developments of organizational reward systems ❑ ❑ ❑
- ☞ Alternative pay systems ❑ ❑ ❑
- ☞ The use and design of incentive and bonus schemes ❑ ❑ ❑
- ☞ The place of an organizational reward scheme in the context of its overall performance management system ❑ ❑ ❑
- ☞ Retention policies and practices. ❑ ❑ ❑

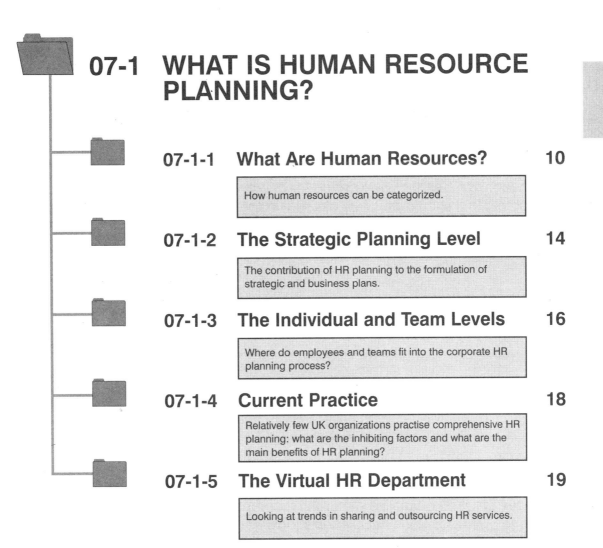

07-1 WHAT IS HUMAN RESOURCE PLANNING?

07-1-1 What Are Human Resources?   10

> How human resources can be categorized.

07-1-2 The Strategic Planning Level   14

> The contribution of HR planning to the formulation of strategic and business plans.

07-1-3 The Individual and Team Levels   16

> Where do employees and teams fit into the corporate HR planning process?

07-1-4 Current Practice   18

> Relatively few UK organizations practise comprehensive HR planning: what are the inhibiting factors and what are the main benefits of HR planning?

07-1-5 The Virtual HR Department   19

> Looking at trends in sharing and outsourcing HR services.

07-1 WHAT IS HUMAN RESOURCE PLANNING?

Any organization which employs (or intends to employ) people will benefit from planning its people requirements, whether deciding how many new employees it will need over a certain time period, or how it will develop its current workforce. This should be a key element in the organization's business plan.

In simple terms, an organization wishing to maximize its human resources planning must:

(1)   Attempt to determine how many people it needs now and in the future

(2)   Determine what knowledge, skills and abilities are needed to ensure the organization can both survive and prosper

(3)   Evaluate the knowledge, skills and abilities of existing employees

(4)   Determine how it will fill the gaps!

In this dossier we concentrate on the *capacity* side of these issues, and explore in depth the practices and procedures effective organizations use to ensure they have the right quantities of human resources in the right places, at the right times. We also consider organizational capability, which is largely to do with the ability of an organization's workforce to achieve the quality of performance required by business objectives. The capability of organizations, teams and individuals is addressed in greater depth in Dossier 04 of this series: *The Learning Organization*.

 ### 07-1-1   What Are Human Resources?

To understand how human resources can be planned, we need to have clear and common understanding of what they are. The term 'employees' can itself be somewhat misleading here.

 **ACTIVITY 1**

In terms of establishing work contracts (i.e. essentially buying labour), employment law distinguishes between two types of service:

(1)   Contracts **of** service

(2)   Contracts **for** services.

Think about what this means and how it applies to your own organization.

Check the definitions in Appendix 1.

The Flexible Firm

We all know that working life is undergoing constant change, with many of the traditional structures and work patterns being replaced by more adaptable and efficient methods. This has been reflected in the way human resources are both obtained and utilized. As early as 1984, John Atkinson recognized the need for flexibility in a competitive business environment. He said this would be composed of three main groups:

(a)   Core workers
(b)   Peripheral workers
(c)   Those employed on a subcontracted basis.

This has been further adapted in the model below:

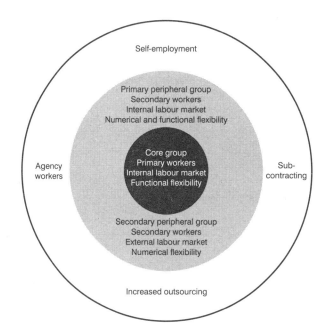

Two separate types of flexibility are identified: *functional* and *numerical.*

The *core workers* are the people employed on standard, permanent, full-time contracts and do the tasks essential to the organization's success. They are *functionally* flexible — that is, they are not tied to rigid job descriptions, but perform a wide range of activities. As well as complex professional and managerial duties, they will also take part in more mundane work, depending on the organization's needs at any particular time.

The *peripheral* group is mainly identified with *numerical* flexibility (although some functional flexibility does exist. This group has been divided into two subgroups:

(a) Primary
(b) Secondary.

The primary group forms part of the firm's internal labour market. These people are mainly full time and primarily permanent, but have lower skills than the core group.

They are less crucial to the firm's success since their skills are widely available in the labour market. They consequently have less job security and will be among the first to have their hours reduced or lose their jobs when downturns are experienced.

The secondary group is in an even less stable position, as they are usually employed to cover short-term needs due to the absence of other staff. They are employed on a part-time or temporary basis.

The last group is made up of people who are not employees (i.e. not under contracts *of* service), but rather hired on a *subcontracted* basis to perform specific tasks (i.e. under contracts *for* services). Their work will mainly be temporary, although their contracts could operate on a *rolling* basis. Some may be professionally qualified and offer specialist services of high value. Some may be employed through agencies. Either way, they will be viewed by the other groups as being outside the organization and easily replaceable if their work becomes unsatisfactory or the services can be obtained more cheaply elsewhere.

07-1

PAUSE TO REFLECT

How do you think the above model applies to your organization? Where do *you* fit in?

It is important to remember that the above is only a model and no two organizations are alike. However, you may find it useful as a framework for planning. The essential point is that Human Resource Planning will often encompass *all* the groups identified.

CASE STUDY:
SHELL INTERNATIONAL EXPLORATION
PRODUCTION

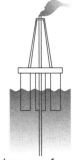

The oil industry is one that has been dominated in recent years by monolithic, vertically integrated giants. However, these companies are now facing challenges from smaller, specialized and more flexible operators, who are able to respond more quickly to market opportunities.

In this changed environment, Shell has created a global pool made up of physically mobile staff and employees with access to a PC who can be virtually mobile. This has been combined with flexible working opportunities in order to attract people into the organization who wish to balance their home and work life while still working for a global organization.

07-1-2   The Strategic Planning Level

The term 'Manpower Planning' has been in common usage for many years. 'Human Resource Planning' is a more recent term. So what's the difference? John Bramham (1994), who has written a great deal on the subject, establishes a firm dichotomy between the two. He views the former as basically quantitative, involving forecasting the demand and supply of labour. He gives the latter a wider meaning, covering plans made across the whole range of personnel and development activity, including 'soft' issues such as motivation, employee attitudes and organizational culture.

Terminology can vary, but we are essentially concerned with looking ahead, using *systematic* techniques to ensure that the organization's labour requirements can be met in the future. That is:

- ☞ The right people
- ☞ With the right skills
- ☞ In the right places
- ☞ At the right time.

Bramham defined Human Resource Planning as '. . . a process whereby courses of action are determined in advance and continually updated, with the aim of ensuring that:

(a)   The organization's demand for labour to meet its projected needs is as accurately predicted as the adoption of modern forecasting techniques allows and

(b)   The supply of labour to the enterprise is maintained by deliberate and systematic action to mobilize it in reasonable balance with these demands.'

The UK's Chartered Institute of Personnel and Development has used the following definition:

'The systematic and continuing process of analysing an organization's human resource needs under changing conditions and developing personnel policies appropriate to the longer-term effectiveness of the organization. It is an integral part of the corporate planning and budgeting procedures since human resource costs and forecasts both affect and are affected by longer-term corporate plans.'

Increasingly, Human Resource Planning is seen as a strategic problem:

☞ It is closely related to, and integrated with, the corporate planning process. Only by aligning the two will the correct priorities and policies be formulated. Much of this will depend on the capability of both the HR professionals and other key decision-makers. It follows that if the corporate plans are either not underpinned with sound market data and projections, or if forecasts are produced on an ad hoc, piecemeal basis, then the HR plans will reflect these with equally substandard outcomes. The process is, or should be, systematic and consciously planned, as opposed to something that happens almost accidentally.

☞ The resource needs will have to be assessed in both quantitative and qualitative terms. As with senior staff, the capability dimension of existing staff and those available in the labour market will be important. A plan produced in a vacuum will not be a basis for sustainable resourcing.

☞ It is a continuing process, since the organization and its objectives, and the environment in which it operates, are continually evolving.

☞ It is both short-term and long-term. However, the emphasis needs to be on longer-term growth and survival.

☞ The planned resources will depend on what the organization can finance.

Whether the organization is capital or labour intensive will impact on the above factors. When labour costs form only a small part of total costs then it is possible to be somewhat more relaxed about staffing levels. In reality, though, organizations will virtually always seek to keep labour costs to a minimum.

At a strategic level, an organization must assess its position in relation to its labour markets. Depending on the nature and size of the organization, these markets could be include any of the following:

(a) Local
(b) National
(c) International.

 PAUSE TO REFLECT

What is the geographical extent of your organization's labour market? Is this likely to change in the near or distant future?

The Human Resource Planning process will mainly be used to formulate the data on which action plans can be based, rather than necessarily drawing up those plans. It may, of course, do both.

For example, if a hotel chain is planning to open a new hotel, the planning function would be required to assess how easy it would be for the company to recruit required staff from internal and external sources. This would be based on experience of opening hotels of a similar size. So it covers:

(a)   Assessing the environment
(b)   Assimilating the data needed to plan the direction the organization needs to take.

As with other forms of corporate planning, its aim is to help the organization achieve its goals — it is not an isolated academic exercise.

 ### 07-1-3   The Individual and Team Levels

In its generally accepted sense, Human Resource Planning is a strategic role. It therefore relies on timely and accurate data from teams, units or departments.

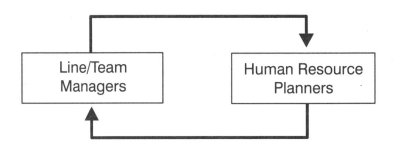

Line managers are the key link between operational teams and strategic planners. They will feed information to the planners regarding their own teams (existing skills/labour turnover/training requirements, etc.). In turn, Human Resource planners will feed back data on the organization as a whole. This should enable interdepartmental comparisons, identify skills gaps (and hence training requirements) and facilitate movement of employees within the organization — i.e. shifting resources to areas of greatest need.

In highly automated companies much of the required data is captured via computer systems, with line managers inputting the required information for the Human Resource planners to collate centrally and then disseminate the key statistics.

Individual career plans will be made at the *micro* level, which will then flow into the *macro* level corporate plan. Often these will be formulated at the annual appraisal which is still favoured by many organizations. Usually line managers and employees will agree individual development needs in the context of the employee's work role and career ambitions. Many enlightened organizations do this on an ongoing basis, to ensure a constant two-way dialogue with staff and to continually feed new requirements into the overall corporate plan. The agreement and *psychological contract* established between the individual and the employer will normally be documented for future review. Many organizations now use some form of developmental 'passport' which the individual retains over a long period to record their assessed and certificated skills and qualifications.

Succession planning, like appraisals, is a basic organizational concept and practice which has been with us for many years, but again is often under-utilized or ignored. The technique is mainly associated with hierarchical organizations where individuals progress their careers by moving upwards and sideways over a number of years as they increase their skills and knowledge base. The basic aim is to ensure an organization has a good enough supply of people coming through the ranks to fill its senior and other key posts. Rothwell's (1995) research indicated that three candidates are typically identified for each senior position:

- ☞ Someone who is ready now and could succeed immediately, if asked to do so
- ☞ Someone who will be ready, if required, in two to three years' time
- ☞ Someone who will be ready in five years' time.

A question to be asked is 'can we find suitable people outside the organization?'. The ability to do this will have a major impact on the degree to which succession planning is used. An organization will weigh up training and development costs against the costs of recruiting external candidates. Some organizations do, of course, prefer 'new blood' to bring in new ideas and ways of working. This can extend to external succession planning, where an organization tracks the career of an individual to make them an offer when they feel the time is right.

Skills planning is a development which has moved the focus away from people to the demand and supply of future skills. This method predicts the competences that will be needed over, say, the next five years. It leaves open the question of how these resources will be obtained. Referring back to our workforce model, it may develop internal staff, use freelance or temporary staff when required, or outsource part of its operations. This approach is particularly useful in markets which suffer a high degree of turbulence.

07-1-4   Current Practice

Research evidence to date, although not comprehensive, seems to indicate that most organizations do not give the HR planning function a high profile. A 1990 study for the UK's Institute of Personnel and Development (at that time the IPM) showed that only three HR planning activities were performed on a formal and regular basis:

☞ Identification of future training needs
☞ Analysis of labour costs and productivity
☞ Assessment of the need for structural change resulting from business plans.

Less than half carried out formal forecasts of the demand and supply of labour. *Less than 20%* formally monitored HR planning practices.

A further study in 1993 showed that where personnel departments had computer systems, only a third used them for Human Resource Planning.

PAUSE TO REFLECT

The above figures seem disappointing. What reasons can you think of for the lack of uptake?

Some of the reasons often put forward for the lack of Human Resource Planning activity in the UK include:

☞ A preference for managerial judgement over statistical techniques
☞ The view that Human Resource Planning is desirable, but not essential
☞ A short-termist outlook in UK business
☞ Practical difficulties associated with inadequate historical data on which to base forecasts
☞ Lack of knowledge of Human Resource Planning techniques
☞ A general ignorance or fear of mathematical models or methods.

These factors are not unique to the UK. Few US or European companies prioritize Human Resource Planning.

 **ACTIVITY 2**

What do you see as the key benefits of Human Resource Planning to your organization? Note down your ideas in about 50 words.

Compare your response with our commentary in Appendix 1.

Whatever methods and techniques an organization uses to perform its Human Resource Planning, it has to ask fundamental questions about the value and cost effectiveness of the process, namely:

☛ Does the inclusion of long-term HR planning significantly contribute to the fulfilment of organizational objectives?

☛ Does the function justify its existence in cost-benefit terms?

☛ What would have been the results for the organization in recent years if such a function had/had not existed?

☛ How does the organization's performance (however that might be measured) compare against similar organizations that have more/less sophisticated methods of HR planning?

07-1-5   The Virtual HR Department

A fundamental decision for organizations today is whether they outsource any parts of the enterprise regarded as 'non-core' — primarily functions such as catering, security, payroll and facilities management, which outside agencies can provide for a fee (often having their own staff on the premises of the host organization). This is something that can affect all, or parts, of the HR function. Indeed, the functions just mentioned often fall under the umbrella of HR. The increasing sophistication of technology, particularly email and the Internet, has substantially increased the viability of this option. A 'halfway house' is when organizations combine their services for mutual benefit.

CASE STUDY:
ANDERSEN CONSULTING

In mid 2000, Andersen Consulting announced that it was to join forces with BT to deliver HR services electronically to other large businesses, resulting in the redeployment of HR staff, if not redundancies.

Judging that there would be a boom in HR outsourcing, the two companies planned to use the 1,100 people in BT's internal HR service centres with Andersen's contacts and e-commerce capabilities to produce a rival to the American-owned company Exult. The resultant firm, peopleSERVE, would also provide HR services to both parent groups. Andersen's payroll and pensions were already handled by a European finance and IT service centre established in Dublin in 1998. BT already had a pensions service centre in Chesterfield, UK. This would be leased out to the new joint venture, together with BT's other UK HR centres in London, Milton Keynes and Stone, Staffordshire.

The service will include the administration of recruitment and selection, training & development, performance management, reward, contracts, retirements and resignations. Because the companies are so large, they have had to seek European Union regulatory approval.

The above example is often referred to as a *shared service*, rather than total outsourcing. In most cases administrative tasks are covered, but sometimes these are outsourced or provided locally. A shared service centre will often supply information and advice on HR policy and practice to operational managers via a call centre and/or intranet. Most organizations which have so far taken this path have retained a core HR group to concentrate on high-level policy and strategy.

The Institute for Employment Studies (IES Report 368) examined 15 organizations and found three prime reasons for introducing shared services:

☞ *Cost cutting*. Economies of scale allow headcount reductions, savings on accommodation charges, streamlining services and utilizing greater buying power.
☞ *Quality improvements*. This includes consistency in service delivery, and being more aware of best practice and sensitive to customer needs.
☞ *Responding to/leading organizational change*. HR is repositioned as a more strategic function, less encumbered by administration. This helps in improving organizational earning across boundaries, for example.

Technology has sometimes been seen as a driver of change, particularly when a new computer system was installed, but more often it has been an enabler.

07-1

CASE STUDY:
HR CALL CENTRE

AskHR is IBM's service centre covering Europe, the Middle East and Africa (EMEA). It provides advice on a call-centre basis. But far from 'dumbing-down' what is provided, it contains a highly skilled pool of employees, with eleven languages being spoken. They are divided into basic grade 'generalists' who take most of the calls, spending around 85% of their time on the phones, and 'specialists' who only use the headsets for about 30% of their time.

IBM's decision to move HR to a single centre was made largely to cut costs. By mid-1999, 90,000 customers in 15 countries were being served by AskHR. IBM also wanted to separate strategic issues from day-to-day work. Additionally, there was an organizational reason. HR was a country-based function supporting an international business divided into customer-facing units. The change split the remaining employees into strategic HR partners serving business teams, and specialists reporting to a process owner, such as head of recruitment. Both structures cover the EMEA region.

Outsourcing – brave new world or urban myth?

It seems from a recent study that the much talked of boom in HR outsourcing may be largely hype. The 'Trends in HR Outsourcing' study (run by Cranfield School of Management in conjunction with the William M Mercer Consultancy) published in the summer of 2000, covered 3,964 large and medium-sized organizations across Europe. It said that 40% did not report any increase in the use of external HR providers over the previous 3 years. Professor Chris Brewster comments:

'It's not very different from 10 years ago. Organizations were using a lot of external suppliers then, and they are still using a lot — but more or less the same amount'.

The study showed that organizations across Europe made considerable use of external providers, especially for training and development and recruitment and selection. This practice was most popular in France, Belgium and the Netherlands, but in all countries it seemed to be used opportunistically, rather than strategically.

It also seems that the term 'outsourcing' has pejorative connotations, implying to some people that an organization was not looking after its people.

However, the report still predicted much larger growth in the use of external providers. Much of this will be driven by the requirement for outside expertise, particularly in using intranet technology for HR and by an increasing tendency for organizations to distinguish between core and non-core activities.

ASP alternatives

HR departments now also have the opportunity of effectively outsourcing their IT systems through Application Service Providers — that is, agents offering a complete package of system functionality, maintenance, data storage, reporting tools, upgrades and helpdesk facilities. Access to such a system is normally via the Internet or an ISDN/modem link. Instead of buying systems software, organizations pay a monthly or quarterly fee to the ASP.

As well as minimal capital outlay and not requiring in-house IT expertise, ASPs offer software opportunities across a range of functions that might not be economical for the client to buy — such as legal advice, occupational health recording and psychometric testing. HR departments need to know, though, that the data is fully secure so many are holding back at present.

An idea of the cost-effectiveness is given by the arrival of OneClickHR.com which will apparently offer services free to smaller companies, with larger organizations being charged around £1 per employee per month.

07-2 PLANNING THE WORKFORCE

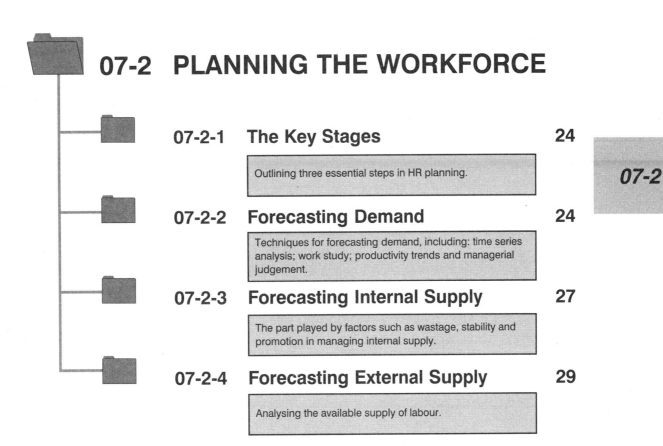

07-2-1 **The Key Stages** **24**

Outlining three essential steps in HR planning.

07-2-2 **Forecasting Demand** **24**

Techniques for forecasting demand, including: time series analysis; work study; productivity trends and managerial judgement.

07-2-3 **Forecasting Internal Supply** **27**

The part played by factors such as wastage, stability and promotion in managing internal supply.

07-2-4 **Forecasting External Supply** **29**

Analysing the available supply of labour.

07-2

07-2 PLANNING THE WORKFORCE

07-2-1 The Key Stages

There are essentially three stages to the Human Resource Planning process:

(1) Assessing what demand the organization will have for people and skills as its business plans are actioned

(2) Forecasting supply based on analysis of internal and external trends and conditions

(3) Assessing the gap between demand and supply to forecast the extent to which additional skills and knowledge will have to be acquired.

In this part of the dossier, we will concentrate on techniques to support the first two stages.

07-2-2 Forecasting Demand

 ACTIVITY 3

What other factors does your organization take into account when forecasting demand? There are two critical factors we haven't mentioned so far.

Compare your suggestions with our commentary in Appendix 1.

Most of the systematic statistical methods used to forecast demand have been based on the following principle:

> *Past experience + current experience = future needs*

Three approaches have been identified: time series analysis, work study, and productivity analysis.

(1) **Time series analysis.** This involves looking at historical business patterns, at the number of people employed in certain occupational categories, and extrapolation to arrive at future estimates. This approach needs a stable environment to be successful. For example, central government should be able to estimate how many geriatric nursing staff will be required in future years, based on demographic trends. Taking all known factors into account, it extrapolates the trend to provide the target figure. Whether this target will be met may, though, be dependent on the supply side — i.e. whether the required number of trained staff will be available in the external market in any given year. However, central government is also in a position to begin the recruitment of trainees to meet that future need.

Time series analysis is useful in industries which are subject to regular cyclical changes. The holiday and leisure sector is a prime example, with hotels having their greatest demand for staff at certain times of the year — during the summer and at Christmas in most cases.

Although this technique is theoretically simple, in practice large organizations would have to perform separate time series for different departments and categories of staff. It is unsuitable for smaller organizations and for fast moving business environments.

(2) **Work study.** This technique is useful when there are no historical trends to look at or totally new business projects or processes are being planned. With this method, instead of relying on past trends for guidance on future developments, special studies are carried out on individual activities to gauge how many people will be required to carry them out effectively. This has normally been most applicable to manufacturing industry where new processes are observed during the development stages and the most effective production method is adopted.

A major drawback of work study is that it can only be used to measure standard tasks. Difficulties arise when attempts are made to measure non-standard tasks, such as the time taken to find faults in equipment.

Work study engineers have to assess the rate at which operators work — a process known as effort-rating. Effort is measured in terms of 'standard performance' — that which should be reached by a qualified and motivated worker, without overexertion. All the operators studied are given an effort-rating relative to this standard.

British Standard Institution (BSI) formulas are shown as either 100/133 or 75/100, where 100 or 75 is average performance without an incentive and 133 or 100 is the performance of a fully motivated operator. Performance ratings are calculated by the formula:

$$\frac{\textit{Number of units produced per day} \times \textit{standard minutes per unit}}{\textit{Actual time taken, in minutes per day}} \times 100$$

So in a working day of 8 hours (480 minutes) an operator may produce 115 units. If the standard time to produce each unit is 5 standard minutes, the rating would be:

$$\frac{\textit{(day's units) } 115 \times \textit{(standard minutes) } 5}{\textit{(actual minutes) } 480} \times 100 = \frac{575}{480} \times 100$$
$$= 119.79$$

(3) **Time series analysis coupled with productivity trends.** Here, improvements in productivity over past years are factored into the calculations and projected to future years. Essentially it removes the assumption that the ratio of staff to work will remain constant over time. It is probably best suited to industries which are able to plan over a long time period.

All three of these techniques suffer the limitation of being time-intensive activities which become less meaningful as the numbers get smaller. Many organizations, particularly small- and medium-sized enterprises (SMEs) prefer to rely on *management judgement* rather than systematic analysis. It does have certain advantages:

☞ Speed
☞ 'Non-scientific' factors such as changes in fashion can be considered
☞ The opinions of a wide number of managers can be pooled.

It may be useful to combine both systematic techniques and managerial judgement. Leap and Crino (1993) give an example of such a formula:

$$E = \frac{(L + G)\ 1/X}{Y}$$

It's not as bad as it looks!

E = number of staff needed at a specific future date.
L = current level of turnover (financial that is, not staff).
G = anticipated growth in turnover.
X = the productivity improvement anticipated during the planning period.
Y = the amount of turnover divided by the number of staff.

PAUSE TO REFLECT

Try applying the formula yourself.

A financial services company is assessing how many staff it will need by the year 2007. It currently employs 1,100.

L is £50.25 M	(current turnover)
G is £7.4 M	(growth in turnover)
X is 1.03	(expected improvement in turnover of 3%)
Y is £45,681	(turnover per member of staff)

So how many staff will it need in 2007?

1,224.15 staff will be needed. Don't be too despondent if you didn't get it quite right — it's looking a long way into the future and as the great economist J M Keynes stated: 'In the long run we are all dead!'.

If you work in the public sector, you may be affected by a very different type of planning: *resource-based provision.* Governments are continually seeking higher levels of productivity, but simultaneously have to consider what the electorate are willing to pay. So with this method of planning they *start* with a budget and then work backwards to decide how many and what type of staff they can afford.

07-2-3   Forecasting Internal Supply

As with forecasting demand, both statistical techniques and management judgement are involved. Detail is important, as figures for overall staff turnover are not tremendously helpful, other than for a crude overview. We need to know about particular groups of people — for example in relation to age bands and skill sets.

 **ACTIVITY 4**

Predicting staff turnover can be difficult, since people leave their jobs for a wide variety of reasons. What reasons for leaving a job are you aware of? You should have at least eight.

Compare your suggestions against ours in Appendix 1.

Two common methods of predicting staff turnover (or 'wastage' as it is often referred to) are *wastage analysis* and *stability analysis.*

Wastage analysis. This index is one of the prime formulae used by Human Resource planners to calculate turnover as a percentage of total population.

$$\frac{Number\ of\ leavers\ in\ a\ specific\ period}{Average\ number\ employed\ in\ the\ same\ period} \times 100$$

Caution is advised with this technique. The overall figure may hide great differences between different parts of the organization and between different categories of staff. For example, empirical data collected over many years has indicated that, *in general terms*:

☛ Wastage rates fall with increasing length of service
☛ Wastage rates fall with increasing age
☛ Wastage rates fall with increasing levels of skill and responsibility
☛ Wastage rates fall when general unemployment rises
☛ Wastage rates are higher for female than for male staff.

 PAUSE TO REFLECT

Consider the people you know (include yourself in this), both family and immediate work colleagues. Do their careers to date follow a pattern indicated by the above factors?

Stability analysis. This technique utilizes wastage rates more effectively.

$$\frac{Number\ of\ employees\ with\ x\ years'\ service\ at\ a\ given\ date}{Number\ employed\ x\ years\ ago} \times 100$$

So, if a business employs 10,000 people at the start of a year and calculates that at the end of the year 9,000 are still in their jobs, it would have a stability rate of 90%.

Essentially, this method examines turnover from a different perspective — concentrating on the proportion of human resources retained, rather than on the numbers lost.

Other methods exist for analysing internal supply, including *cohort analysis,* which chooses a specific group of staff recruited together and looks at the 'survival rate' over time. This is useful for homogeneous groups, such as sales teams or management trainees. *Internal promotion analysis* is used to predict staff flows within the organization, based on historical data. This is perhaps only really useful in large organizations with very defined structures (and the pace of change today means that such hierarchical structures normally last no more than a couple of years).

 ### 07-2-4   Forecasting External Supply

In most organizations a gap will exist between demand for staff and the internal supply. This has to be plugged from outside.

Some internal information may be useful for evaluating the potential external supply, in terms of both quantity and quality. This may take the form of the response rates to advertisements, the quality of interviewees and the number of staff leaving to join other organizations. However, the most useful information will be collected from outside the organization.

Most labour markets are local, based on a 'travel to work' area (often determined by time, rather than distance, as a motorway or good train service can substantially increase the distance people are willing to commute). It is important for the Human Resource planner to gather a number of key statistics, including:

- ☞ Unemployment rates
- ☞ Population density
- ☞ Number of school leavers
- ☞ Proportion with or in higher education
- ☞ Skill levels
- ☞ Age profile (e.g. seaside towns are often retirement havens).

The question of available skills is an interesting challenge facing organizations starting new plants on 'greenfield' sites. Do they move to an area near to their competitors, so they can 'poach' people who already have the skills they need, or do they start-up in a location without immediate competitors and train the local population? There are pluses and minuses with both:

Near competitors	+	Can buy in skills immediately and start full production quickly.
	–	Could incur greater costs as may have to pay high salaries to tempt staff from competitors.
Competitor free	+	More likely to keep wage costs under control.
	–	Will have to go through expensive and possibly lengthy training programme. Full production delayed.

The market data collected by Human Resource planners will therefore need to be accurate and up-to-date, to avoid costly errors.

CASE STUDY: TOYOTA

When the Toyota car company decided to start a brand new plant in Derby (UK), buying in existing skills was not a priority. They were less interested in the skills people already had, but rather what type of person they would be. *90% of those recruited had never worked in the industry before.* To give an idea of scale, they received over 35,000 applications, with 9,000 people going through their assessment centre, 5,000 of those being interviewed and 3,000 being appointed.

Another prime value during Toyota's recruitment process was that although it's important to hire the right people, it's even more important to train them — *'even with the right ingredients, you still need to bake the cake'*.

After the initial recruitment exercise, Toyota's emphasis switched to improving efficiency. Their HR specialists are told 'don't let anyone leave, as you can't replace them — you'll have to improve productivity'.

We will give more information on the Toyota recruitment exercise later in this dossier.

Local labour market information can be obtained from a variety of sources, including government publications, chambers of commerce, local authorities and employment agencies.

www.universal-manager.com

To bring together what we have examined in this section, the following diagram provides a useful template. It also adds some additional points to consider, such as the commercial factors which influence planning, and reward systems (which we examine in Section 07-7 of this dossier).

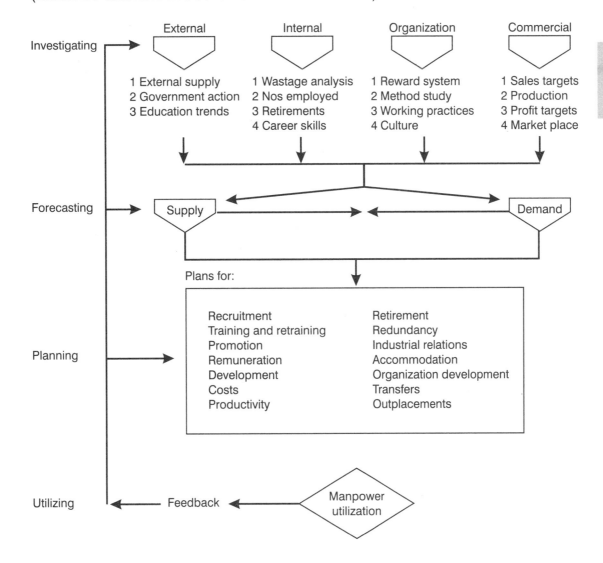

31

07-3 JOB ANALYSIS AND WORKFORCE PROFILING

07-3

07-3-1 Principles of Job Analysis   36

Having looked at the many uses of job analysis, we list five important principles of the discipline.

07-3-2 Methods of Analysis   37

Describing a variety of methods of collecting and analysing data concerning jobs.

07-3-3 Job Descriptions and Person Specifications   41

Two trusted formats in HR management – but how relevant are they today?

07-3-4 Job Families   46

Grouping jobs to support workforce profiling, career planning and reward structures.

07-3 JOB ANALYSIS AND WORKFORCE PROFILING

What is job analysis?

It can be described as a process to determine and describe the content of jobs in such a way that a clear understanding of what any job is about can be communicated to anyone who might require the information for management purposes. You may sometimes hear it referred to as 'occupational analysis', as in the quotation at the foot of this page.

Why is it important?

Job analysis has a central part to play in Human Resource Planning and on a range of practices within the organization. It has a central part to play in:

☞   Recruitment and selection
☞   The determination of pay differentials
☞   The identification of training needs
☞   The setting of performance targets
☞   The construction of new organizational structures.

Additionally, without objective, effective job analysis behind them, it can be very difficult to back up key decisions in such areas as:

☞   Redundancy
☞   Promotion
☞   Disciplinary action
☞   Performance review
☞   Changing rates of pay.

So, although it is primarily a technical and administrative tool, it adds value to a range of the organization's activities. C Legere (1985) has stated that:

Occupational analysis is a business investment — it requires considerable expenditure of funds, human effort and time. These costs, however, can be amortized over a period of time, during which the data can be used to avoid costs, tailor programs, increase efficiency and flexibility, improve quality control, and effect operational change. The data developed during occupational analysis can serve initially to validate existing programs, to document or articulate specific program needs, or to influence almost every aspect of the personnel management program within that occupation'.

Let's look at the help job analysis gives in a number of areas:

☛ **Human Resource Planning.** Organizations have to plan the resources required to meet their agreed objectives. We have already seen that this means having the right people in the right places at the right time. This might mean designing totally new jobs or redesigning existing jobs to meet current or future demands. For these activities it is vital that the organization has good analytical data about its jobs.

☛ **Job evaluation.** This is one of the standard reasons for undertaking job analysis. If the information used is not accurate, it will not produce fair results and could undermine the credibility of the procedure.

☛ **Selection.** The organization must have clear information about what skills, knowledge, experience, attitude and personal attributes are needed for each job — otherwise it cannot properly match potential candidates against these. Job descriptions and person specifications will be drawn-up for this purpose (see Section 07-6 'Recruitment and Selection').

☛ **Organization review.** When structures are being amended it is necessary to have sound information about the content of jobs. This will ensure that any important tasks are not overlooked and duplication doesn't occur.

☛ **Training and development.** Analytical information allows outputs to be matched to the knowledge, competences and skills required for each job and, from them, the training and development needs for each individual and team.

☛ **Job redesign.** We know that organizations are changing very rapidly both in terms of operations and structure. Reallocating duties and redesigning jobs therefore has to be carried out quickly. Good information about jobs will allow this to be completed quickly and effectively.

☛ **Employee rights.** A job description of some kind should be given to each employee, so that there is no ambiguity about what each role entails and the outputs required from it. If this isn't clear, it could lead to issues of performance, discipline and grievance. The job description is a prime part of the contractual relationship between employer and employee — the employer who doesn't clearly state what the job is about could be storing up trouble for the future.

☛ **Performance management.** To ensure employees are performing their jobs to their maximum effectiveness, to the benefit of both individuals and organization, comprehensive information is needed. The requirements of the job can then be compared with the extent to which the individual meets those requirements.

07-3

07-3-1   Principles of Job Analysis

The principles governing job analysis are:

(1) **Jobs, not people,** are analysed. The skills, knowledge and experience required for the job itself should not be confused with those of the current postholder (there may of course be a gap between the two). It is always worth remembering that there are a variety of factors that can affect job content, as illustrated below.

(2) **Non-judgemental.** The person carrying out the job analysis should not be concerned with how appropriate each part of the job is — i.e. personally, they might think the whole job is a complete waste of time, but it is not their role to comment, unless they have been asked to perform some kind of organizational review.

(3) **Not a list of tasks.** The analysis should describe the various components of the role and how it relates to the success of the organization. Simply listing individual tasks will only provide a partial picture and will not give the job 'life'.

(4) **Here and now.** The analysis should concentrate on the job as it is today, rather than anything that may have happened to it in the past, or any potential future changes.

(5) **A tool.** Job analysis is a process, a means to an end, not an end in itself.

07-3-2   Methods of Analysis

There is a variety of different approaches to job analysis and we will attempt here to give a flavour of what is available.

 ## PAUSE TO REFLECT

What do you think will influence the technique chosen to perform the analysis?

The technique chosen will depend on the type of information being looked for. If training and development is driving job analysis, then the analysis will not just concentrate on individual tasks, but also on the skills and resources used.

Questionnaires

Collecting data about jobs via a structured questionnaire has the advantages of reducing time and cost. Where large numbers of current job holders are to be consulted, a well-designed questionnaire will generate clear and useful findings. By using a structured questioning approach a good level of consistency can be obtained.

The *Position Analysis Questionnaire (PAQ)*, one of a number of commercial packages available, gathers six discrete categories of information:

(1)   The source of information used to do the job (how and where the employee gets the information)
(2)   The kind of mental processes required (reasoning, decision-making, planning)
(3)   The output expected and methods used (physical activities performed, tools and equipment used)
(4)   The types and levels of relationships with others
(5)   The physical and social environment in which the job is performed
(6)   Additional job characteristics and activities not covered by the above — such as hours and level of responsibility.

This reiterates that job analysis is not just concerned with data on job content, but how each job fits into the organization, what its purpose is, and the skills and personality traits needed to perform it.

Interviews

With this common method, *trained* analysts talk to the job holder, relevant supervisors and colleagues about the job and how it fits into the organization. The job holder is encouraged to be open and discuss particular events they have experienced. What they say is then validated by others.

PAUSE TO REFLECT

With this method, what do you think the inherent weakness may be? How might it be overcome?

There is a strong possibility that the interviewee will 'talk up' their work to impress the interviewer (particularly if a regrading is being considered). They will tend to concentrate on the more interesting aspects and downplay the mundane duties. It is common for people to think they have more responsibility than is the case, particularly if they've had a little responsibility delegated to them.

It is often better to interview staff who have been in the job for a relatively short period of time, rather than those who have been in it for many years. A trained interviewer will, however, be able to 'bring back' the employee to the nitty-gritty details of their work.

A good way of ameliorating this problem is to conduct a group interview of several people in the same role. There is then less chance that one person will exaggerate. As stated earlier, it is important to remind them that it is the job that is being analysed, not the person's performance in it.

 ## ACTIVITY 5

Imagine you have to conduct a job analysis interview in two weeks' time in a department you don't know much about. What things would you have to do or consider before, during and after the interview? List 10 below.

(1)

(2)

(3)

(4)

(5)

(6)

(7)

(8)

(9)

(10)

Compare your list against our points in Appendix 1.

Several specific job analysis interviewing methods have been developed to strengthen the process. Two of them are:

☞ Critical Incident Technique
☞ The Repertory Grid.

(1)   Critical Incident Technique

Here the job holder is asked only to concentrate on those aspects of the job that make the difference between success and failure. The starting point is objectives, with the interviewer agreeing and recording the main inputs and outputs required in the job to produce the desired performance levels. Once these are established, the next step in the interview process is to get the post holder to describe actual incidents (hence the title) or events that resulted in success or failure in meeting key objectives. They are asked to state specifically what their own contribution to the outcome was.

This technique helps to avoid recording general statements and gives the interviewer a very detailed picture of the role. The behaviours required for success are comprehensively documented.

A variant of critical incident technique is *hierarchical task analysis*. Jobs are broken down into a hierarchical set of tasks and then into subtasks. These are then described in terms of their inputs, outputs and how they are to be achieved. The process details what has to be done, the standards to attain and any specific conditions associated with performing the tasks.

(2)   The Repertory Grid

This involves putting together a list of tasks that form part of a job and then comparing each one with all the others with regard to the skills and abilities needed for success. Pairs or trios of tasks are chosen at random. These are then analysed by the job holder, supervisor and colleagues to establish new information on the pertinent skills.

The list of tasks and skills are then positioned at right-angles to each other on a grid. This allows each skill to be rated in terms of its significance to the achievement of each task. A five or seven point rating scale is normally used, with a score of one meaning that the skill is not relevant to the task and a five or seven meaning that it is crucial.

A simple example for a telesales agent is given below.

Duties	Skills				
	Assertiveness	*Accuracy*	*Keyboard skills*	*Reliability*	*Verbal fluency*
Make outbound calls	5	2	1	4	4
Record customer details	2	5	4	4	2
Complete sale	4	5	2	4	4
Forward documentation	1	4	2	5	1

Here is a rundown of some of the available options for collecting data to support job analysis.

(a)   Self-reports
This approach involves post holders describing their roles and producing job descriptions. It can lead to substantial discrepancies and variations between employees both in content and accuracy (not least because of differences in writing skills). Thorough training is usually needed to make self-reporting work — particularly if it is to be used as the basis for grading and, hence, pay.

(b)   Diaries and logs
Here the post holder is required to keep a full record of what they do each day. It can be a time-consuming approach and is rarely suitable for people in repetitive or predictable jobs. It is again open to a high degree of subjectivity and needs to take place in a non-threatening work environment.

(c)   Checklists
These tend to be of most use when there are a large number of jobs with a relatively straightforward task breakdown. A long list of tasks is given to the post holder and/or supervisor and they tick off the ones used in the job.

(d)   Observation
Tends to be regarded as one of the most accurate, but at the same time costly, methods of gathering job data. It was at the heart of work study methods, which have now largely disappeared. One serious drawback with observation is that the people observed might well change their behaviour — for many years this has been known as the *Hawthorne effect*, following a series of experiments conducted in the USA at the Western Electric Company.

(e)   Participant observation
This involves the analyst actually performing the job and recording their findings. Naturally, it can only really work for either routine jobs or in a section or department where the analyst already knows the work intimately — otherwise the technique will quickly fall into disrepute.

07-3

 ### 07-3-3   Job Descriptions and Person Specifications

The written **job description** has long been the primary output from a job analysis process. It is at the heart of many Human Resource Planning decisions and processes (such as the production of training plans and determination of rates of pay), and supports organizational processes for managing performance. Forming a key part of the contractual package, job descriptions often provide a key defence in cases of unfair discrimination.

 ### PAUSE TO REFLECT

In fact, the job description is a multi-purpose tool. What uses does it have in your organization?

Some typical applications of the job description include:

☞ *As a tool in recruitment*. Help for adverts and briefing applicants.
☞ *As a tool in selection*. Decisions about which candidates to appoint can be made with reference to an up-to-date job description to ensure that other factors (e.g. personal bias) do not cloud the judgements.
☞ *For employment contracts*. Often organizations will make reference to job descriptions in their contracts of employment. They can be important if an employee is dismissed for failing to reach required performance standards. Similarly, if someone resigns and then claims constructive dismissal for being given work outside their terms of employment, the job description's content can make or break the case.
☞ *For communicating values*. Information about the organization's priorities, expectations and rewards can be included to outline what the employee is expected to achieve.

☛ *As a defence against unfair discrimination.* If someone feels that they have been denied employment (or promotion) due to discrimination, and takes legal action against the employer, the job description will be a critical piece of evidence.

The legal points above illustrate not only the value of having a job description, but of getting it right. If nebulous phrases are used, or ones which are all-embracing, the employer's case may be weakened. However, the reverse is true if the requirements in the job description are written clearly, concisely and objectively.

Armstrong (1996) has given some general advice about constructing meaningful job descriptions, as follows:

☛ Each item contained in the job description should relate to the outputs that the job holder will be expected to produce.
☛ The document should make explicit what the job holder can be held responsible for.
☛ If a component task of the job is to be completed under supervision, this should be made clear.
☛ If there are deadlines to be worked to, these should be included.

It is also argued that the language in job descriptions should refer to *what gets done*, rather than *what employees do*, so that ambiguity is reduced.

Job descriptions tend not to vary a great deal in their main headings from organization to organization and usually include:

☛ Job title.
☛ Grade/rate of pay.
☛ Main location.
☛ Supervisor's name/post.
☛ Details of any subordinates.
☛ Main purpose of the job — i.e. a succinct summary of why it exists.
☛ List of the principal duties and accountabilities with brief descriptions. These would not normally number more than around ten, or there will be too much detail. More senior employees will tend to have *objectives* to achieve, rather than *tasks* to carry out.
☛ Reference to other documents (such as trade union or other collective agreements) that may expand on other items.
☛ Context — how work is processed. Where it comes from and goes to, together with any environmental conditions and how it fits into the rest of the organization.
☛ Contacts — communication lines, including external people and bodies, and the reason for them.
☛ Dimensions — financial or statistical information that illustrates job size.
☛ Working conditions — particularly if there are special conditions relating to chemical hazards, noise and so on.

☞ Signatures of post holder and supervisor, plus date — it is surprising how many job descriptions in current use are more than five years old.

Drawbacks of job descriptions include:

☞ The content and quality will depend very much on the job analysis technique used and the skills of the analyst. Weaknesses in either will be transmitted directly to the job description.

☞ If job descriptions are written too rigidly, they can affect flexibility, with employees retorting: *'I'm not doing that, it's not on my job description'.*

☞ It is now widely acknowledged that in today's work environment, job descriptions date fast.

☞ In modern organizations employees can be used very flexibly, according to their abilities, rather than the specific, itemized, duties they were originally hired to perform.

07-3

Person specifications set out the attributes required to perform a particular role. They are used as the basis for shortlisting and selection, and normally specify requirement in terms of:

☞ Skills
☞ Knowledge
☞ Personality attributes
☞ Education and qualifications
☞ Experience.

The individual items listed under each of these headings are then commonly divided into 'desirable' and 'essential'.

There are a number of ways of describing the ideal candidate for a job, with two popular ones being Munro Fraser's Five-Fold Grading System and Alec Rodger's Seven-Point Plan. These are shown below:

Five-Fold Grading System
(1) Impact on others — physical make-up, appearance, speech and manner
(2) Acquired qualifications — educational, vocational training, work experience
(3) Innate abilities — quickness of comprehension and aptitude for learning
(4) Motivation — individual goals, consistency and determination in following them up, success rate
(5) Adjustment — emotional stability, ability to stand up to stress and ability to get on with people.

Seven-Point Plan
(1) Physical make-up — health, appearance, bearing and speech
(2) Attainments — education, qualifications and experience
(3) General intelligence — intellectual capacity
(4) Special aptitudes — mechanical or manual dexterity, facility in use of words and figures
(5) Interests — intellectual, practical, constructional, physical, social, artistic
(6) Disposition — acceptability, influence over others, steadiness, dependability, self-reliance
(7) Circumstances — any special demands of the job, such as ability to work unsocial hours, or travel abroad.

Both models are well-established in HR and should be considered against prevailing legislation. For instance, factor one in each model is likely to contravene the European Human Rights Convention (2000), as it may deny freedom of expression and ask unduly intrusive questions of prospective candidates. This is also true for point five of the Seven-point Plan. Point seven may stray into the area of indirect sexual discrimination, perhaps implying that a woman with a family may not be able to meet these sorts of requirements.

The skill, qualification and experience requirements have to be those that are strictly necessary for effective performance of the job. If any unnecessary factors are included, they might unfairly discriminate against minority groups.

Competences

Some organizations will prefer to emphasize the behavioural competences needed by the post holder. A popular framework for this is the MSL/McBer competence cluster for managerial jobs, as shown below.

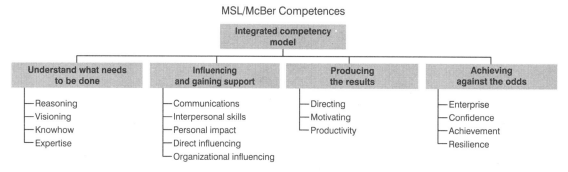

MSL/McBer Competences

Competences have the advantage of describing observable behaviour, which is helpful in assessing work performance. In many organizations there is a competence framework in place providing each work role with a set of clear performance standards and a path for development. But competences need to be defined thoroughly to avoid vagueness or ambiguity and, again, indirect discrimination or human rights infringements. Their definitions should distinguish between excellent, acceptable and unacceptable performance.

PAUSE TO REFLECT

Besides job analysis and definition, what other applications might a framework of competences have?

If an organization puts in place a competence framework, or mechanisms such as performance indicators, it is then able to align the processes of selection, performance, monitoring, reward and discipline designed to bring about and reinforce those behaviours. It is essential that these are aligned properly and that the competences identified are appropriate to the organization. If not, a situation could arise where an individual was recruited against one set of criteria, expected to do something else by his/her colleagues, appraised against another list of indicators and rewarded by an unrelated system.

The standard practice is to start with high performers. Analysis (perhaps using critical incident or repertory grid) aims to ascertain why they are effective and use that knowledge to create a competence framework reflecting the behavioural strategies used by successful people. Organizations will not all use the same competence template, but there now exists a comprehensive 'menu' of competences from which to choose. The culture and values of an organization are important in choosing which competences sit in their framework. For example, a traditional accountancy firm may want auditors who are thorough and trustworthy. By comparison, a small direct sales operation may need people who are driven and opportunistic.

07-3

It is crucial that people within an organization contribute to producing their own competence framework. Those imported wholesale from outside will feel alien and not part of everyday working life — like a ten-page mission statement written solely by the chairman. On the other hand, a keen awareness of the competences required to compete in the organization's environment is crucial. And insularity in devising competences can result in 'cloning', i.e. the recruitment and promotion of people whose close similarities reduce organizational creativity and flexibility.

Organizations should look forwards, not backwards, when drawing up core competences. Some of the competences from the past that have brought success will be valid, but some will be outdated or marginalized.

Competence frameworks are discussed further in Section 07-6 of this dossier.

Minimizing the drawbacks of job analysis

We have already commented on the negative aspects of individual job analysis techniques. None are perfect and neither are the people performing them.

There are, though, a couple of ways in which we can reduce problems:

☛ *Regular updating.* Each line manager should be required to update the job descriptions of reporting positions at least once a year. A good time to do this is before the annual appraisal of the current post holder. The content can then be agreed and signed-off as part of that process.

☛ *Loose job descriptions.* To cope with rapid change, job analysis can be flexible, using less precise language in the job description. For example, instead of stating that a job involves writing monthly sales reports, it could just state: 'providing sales data when required'.

07-3-4 Job Families

A job family is a group of jobs in which the nature and objectives of the work are similar, but the work is performed at different levels. Job family definitions are used to identify levels of competence or capacity within a job family as a basis for rewarding people within that family. The Hay Management Consultants' (1996) process of job family modelling involves:

☛ Identifying the families
☛ Analysing and determining levels of work in each family
☛ Establishing levels of work between job families by job evaluation
☛ Defining pay grades.

Job families can be treated as distinct market groups, with the structure helping career planning, but the system can be divisive and equal pay issues may arise between the families. Where movement between job families is inhibited there is also the danger that people will become 'labelled'.

Jobs within a family may be linked in any of the following ways:

☛ The nature of the work — e.g. customer services
☛ The professional or technical discipline — e.g. engineers or scientists
☛ The same job operating at different levels — e.g. secretaries
☛ A common function — e.g. sales
☛ Branch (or regional) managers — with local conditions reflecting the size of different branches.

An important point relating to the broad-band pay structures associated with job families is that formal analytical job evaluation schemes may not be used at all. If they are used, they may have an essentially supporting role once the band structures have been defined.

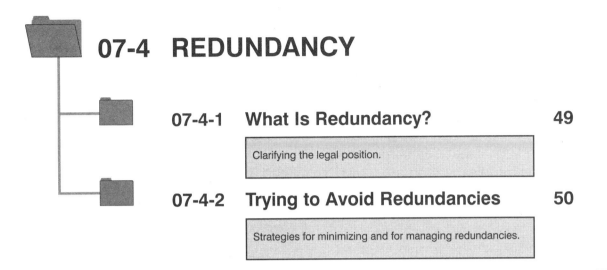

07-4 REDUNDANCY

07-4-1 **What Is Redundancy?** 49

Clarifying the legal position.

07-4-2 **Trying to Avoid Redundancies** 50

Strategies for minimizing and for managing redundancies.

07-4

07-4 REDUNDANCY

It is perhaps not surprising that we may tend to think of Human Resource Planning in terms of positive events, such as how to plan recruitment, train the workforce, and cope with expansion. But there are negative elements involved in planning — that is, ensuring that if a problem arises, its impact is minimized and the people involved are treated fairly and with dignity. Redundancy planning is one such activity.

. . . that the people involved are treated fairly and with dignity!

The three main routes out of an organization are resignation, retirement and redundancy. Although in this section we will be covering redundancies and practices connected with redundancy programmes, you should bear in mind that 'voluntary' retirements, for employees who have reached a certain age, are often used as an alternative. In reality, pressure is placed on the employee to accept retirement and the associated pension payment as an alternative to a one-off redundancy payment.

We looked at the wide variety of reasons people leave organizations in Activity 4. However, distinguishing between departures initiated by employers and those actioned by employees is not completely straightforward. While some reasons for termination are easy to define, such as dismissal for gross misconduct, or someone resigning to join another organization, others may have a number of contributory factors. Common examples of this blurring occur when someone resigns without having another position or when someone has to retire at a predetermined age, when perhaps they would have preferred to continue working.

07-4-1   What Is Redundancy?

A major point to make is that *jobs are made redundant, not people*. A person's employment may be terminated because their job is disappearing, but strictly speaking the classic comment of 'I'm being made redundant' is incorrect — it should be 'my job is being made redundant'. But this semantic distinction will not make much difference to the despondency of the person affected.

The Employment Protection (Consolidation) Act 1978 stated that a termination due to redundancy occurs due to one of four reasons:

☞ The employer has ceased, or will cease, carrying out the *business* in which the person was employed

☞ The employer has ceased, or will cease, carrying out the *business* at the *place* where the person was employed

☞ The requirement to perform a *particular type of work* has ceased or diminished and the person was employed in that work

☞ The requirement to perform a *particular type of work* has ceased or diminished at the *place* where the person was employed.

07-4

So if there has not been a reduction in the overall need for staff in general, or at a particular location, then, in legal terms, a redundancy has not occurred.

 ACTIVITY 6

> What do you think this means for organizations that are expanding? Does it mean no jobs can be made redundant?

Compare your initial thoughts against our comments in Appendix 1.

You may at first feel that the legal definition is rather academic, but it can be critical for a number of reasons, not least financial. For example, there are minimum guaranteed redundancy payments and the Inland Revenue allows a certain amount of redundancy pay to be paid tax-free. You should remember that redundancies are just one type of dismissal and Employment Tribunals will always look to ensure that proper procedures have been followed and that, as is mentioned elsewhere in this dossier, a *'reasonable' approach is taken.*

Part of the process of examining reasonableness would be to see what steps had been taken to avoid the redundancies, whether the correct procedures had been followed and the relevant redundancy payments made. So let's look at the practicalities.

07-4-2   Trying to Avoid Redundancies

 ACTIVITY 7

What long-term approach might your organization (or any other) take to minimize redundancy?

Compare your answer with our comments in Appendix 1.

Fowler (1993) gave three areas in which managers could avoid compulsory redundancies, each involving planning. The first we have covered in the above Activity. The second is . . .

Flexible Working Practices

If it is known that certain types of work are to disappear (as part of business forecasting), it may be possible for the employees affected to develop new job roles. Fowler makes a distinction between:

☛ *'organizational flexibility'*, meaning cutting down the hierarchy and setting up multifunctional teams, and
☛ *'job flexibility'*, which means enriching individual jobs so that employees become multiskilled.

 PAUSE TO REFLECT

What does this actually mean in terms of redundancy avoidance? What is the link?

It creates more efficient organizations in which the employees become increasingly adaptable to changing circumstances. In simple terms, instead of bringing in new workers to do the new jobs, the organization can use the existing workers to do the new jobs.

In the last activity we referred to the utilization of temporary staff. Another, related option is *'outsourcing'*, which takes us back to our earlier model of 'the flexible firm'. This means employing, for certain tasks, external subcontractors. An example might be if a major new computer system is to be installed: rather than employ its own staff for, say, 12 months, the organization will use staff from another firm — often this is the same firm that supplies the hardware. So if the organization doesn't use staff on *contracts of service,* it won't have to make them redundant in due course.

A word of warning!

It has become something of a standing joke in a number of organizations that the easiest way to double your earnings is to take early retirement or be made redundant — then return the next month as a 'consultant'. In fact, many organizations have pursued this path. That is, they have employed former staff on projects, paying them on a 'freelance' basis and followed this up with successive short-term contracts, possibly over a number of years.

Welcome back Fred, here's your first consultation fee!

This is a potentially hazardous approach. Firstly, if the employee's job had been made redundant and then she/he is re-employed in a similar capacity, there is the possibility of a later claim being made for unfair dismissal, since the job still exists. The second problem concerns the Inland Revenue, which now has strict rules on what being a 'consultant' or 'self-employed' means. Questions to be asked include: is the person registered as a company for VAT purposes and does she/he work for a number of different organizations? If, in effect, the person only works for one organization and this employment lasts for a lengthy period of time, the Revenue will regard them as an employee of that organization, which will have to pay National Insurance contributions for that employee over the period of their employment.

Early Retirement

This is often a favourite way to avoid redundancies, as Inland Revenue rules allow organizations to retire people at 50 years of age with enhanced pensions. It can be popular with those affected for three reasons:

- ☞ They do not just have to make do with a one-off redundancy payment.
- ☞ They receive their pension (albeit at a reduced rate) immediately and for the rest of their life, giving an element of long-term security.
- ☞ They can still attempt to gain full-time or part-time employment elsewhere.

Even though they are described as retired, such people are still being made redundant, except that it is *voluntary* redundancy (although you may wish to debate how much choice some people actually have in the matter).

PAUSE TO REFLECT

Early retirement may sound a good option, but is it an 'ageist' approach?

Of course not everyone over 50 is affected — only a small percentage of those offered the chance may actually accept. Additionally, an organization needs an occupational pension scheme to make the retirement option viable, and volunteers have to be in the scheme to benefit. If the scheme is a contributory one (i.e. members have to contribute some of their own salary — normally 5 or 6%) some people may decide not to bother.

It can sometimes be surprising how few people join their organization's pension scheme, even though they are, in effect, a very efficient investment as the employer will contribute far more to the scheme than the employee. Some schemes are, of course, non-contributory.

At this point, some readers might be thinking 'a pension is a benefit, so what's it got to do with planning?'. Well, in the HR field, in parallel with the national economy, everything affects everything else in some way. In this case:

- ☞ We have already stated that a scheme is necessary for early retirement, which aids the long-term planning process. A non-contributory scheme will undoubtedly mean that more people in the organization are members — hence giving a further planning advantage.
- ☞ Then there is recruitment planning — part of this is 'how do we attract the people we want?' A key aspect of this is the overall benefits package on offer. Not having a pension scheme could easily deter applicants in times of tight labour markets.

Other Strategies

We have established that early retirement may not always be an option. Even if it is compulsory, redundancies may still be unavoidable. So what else can be done? Well, the next obvious step is to ask for volunteers. This request will normally be 'sweetened' with an enhanced leaving package. Some people may find this an attractive option, particularly if they were already thinking about a move or have highly transferable skills.

Asking for volunteers sounds, superficially, a straightforward and reasonable option. However, it is riddled with potential handicaps:

☞ If a lot of people volunteer, the organization may let poorer performers go, for obvious reasons, while the better ones are left to continue work until normal retirement age. This could breed resentment in those who were not chosen, as they would feel that poorer workers had been rewarded (particularly if they received enhanced severance payments).

☞ If long-serving employees volunteer, the organization (as well as losing some of its 'cream' employees) will face a hefty financial payout, as payments (statutory *and* employer-enhanced) are based on length of service.

☞ If the more able employees volunteer, then the organization could be compounding its problems in the long run. It has less chance of pulling out of any difficulties with less able people at its disposal.

☞ 'Blotting the copybook'. Some employees may be deterred from volunteering if there is a chance of being unsuccessful. They may feel that an application for early retirement will be interpreted as a lack of commitment, which may inhibit their future career prospects within the organization.

 PAUSE TO REFLECT

Spend a few minutes considering how these pitfalls might be avoided.

Often when a company needs to 'lose' a large number of employees quickly (e.g. following a merger, company purchase or the loss of a major order or market), it will offer voluntary redundancy across the board — the short-term aim is purely to cut the head count and slash the payroll.

However, if it is not faced with such a dramatic scenario, there are other options:

- ☛ Targeting specific departments or grades. This may apply if the organization wishes to 'de-layer'; that is, reduce the number of hierarchical levels. Many organizations have carried out this process in recent years, and quite a few have suffered from its limiting effect on promotional and succession-planning opportunities.
- ☛ Targeting poor performers, perhaps prior to taking the offer of voluntary redundancy to a wider audience. This targeting, where appropriate, would probably include the early retirement option. If only a limited number of people were approached to begin with, it would also not unduly raise expectations in other groups.
- ☛ A freeze on recruitment. This runs normally for a limited period — perhaps 3, 6 or 12 months. During that time employees may leave through natural wastage, so when the 'day of judgement' arrives, the need for voluntary or compulsory redundancies may be reduced or even made unnecessary. If this causes short-term problems in some areas, the organization can either action internal transfers (temporary or permanent) or bring in agency staff. Retraining opportunities will also be more viable.
- ☛ Reducing other staff costs. As well as a freeze on standard pay, this can include reducing or stopping overtime, weekend working, bonus schemes, profit-related pay, free parking and so on. It may necessitate a change in accommodation or moving to a new site — perhaps selling the old premises and moving to rented or leased accommodation.

When such action has to be implemented, it is so much more effective if employees are 'on-board' from the start of the process — constant, open communication is the first rule of any major change programme.

Although the UK has existing statutory requirements relating to consultation over redundancies, enlightened organizations will go much further. They know that if employees feel they are not being kept in the dark and are treated consistently, they will be more willing to be flexible in helping with whatever remedial action is necessary. If trade unions are recognized by the organization, their representatives would normally be intimately involved in the discussions and negotiations. Once again, though, as with other Human Resource areas, the emphasis should be on planning rather than reacting.

Don't keep employees in the dark!

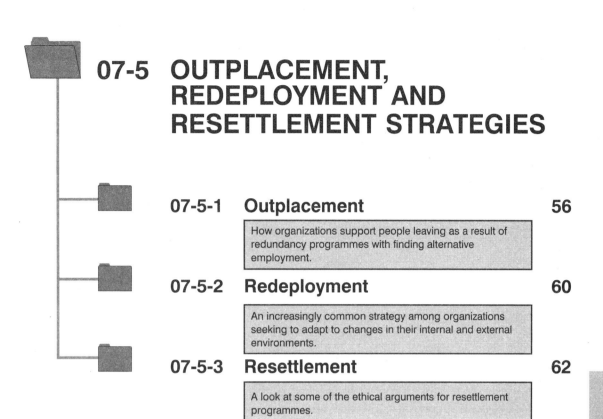

07-5 OUTPLACEMENT, REDEPLOYMENT AND RESETTLEMENT STRATEGIES

07-5-1 Outplacement 56

How organizations support people leaving as a result of redundancy programmes with finding alternative employment.

07-5-2 Redeployment 60

An increasingly common strategy among organizations seeking to adapt to changes in their internal and external environments.

07-5-3 Resettlement 62

A look at some of the ethical arguments for resettlement programmes.

07-5

07-5 OUTPLACEMENT, REDEPLOYMENT AND RESETTLEMENT STRATEGIES

In the previous section you got to grips with redundancy and how to manage it. We now turn to a discussion of three ways in which the progressive, caring organization can 'help those chosen for redundancy'.

07-5-1 Outplacement

Outplacement is a recent addition to the HR lexicon. It usually involves making use of career consultants to help those being made redundant to find alternative employment. In large-scale redundancies, the organization may not be able to cope itself with providing the necessary support for those affected — and it will probably be the case that the HR department has also been cut in size, so some of its members will be looking for help rather than giving it.

The assistance provided by outplacement consultants is not, of course, an act of charity. They can charge substantial fees, especially if senior staff are involved. The costs, though, will be offset against (a) future savings in salary and benefit payments to redundant staff and (b) positive public relations both within and outside the organization.

The Services on Offer

The extent (and quality) of outplacement support depends mainly on what the sponsoring organization is prepared to pay. The following services are typically offered:

☛ **Preparing CVs or application forms**. Someone who has applied for a lot of jobs may feel this is straightforward. However, some of the people being made redundant may not have had to apply for work for a long time. They may even have acquired their job informally — perhaps as a relative of an existing employee, or by extending a temporary contract. Often the most senior people have particular difficulty — it might be up to 30 years since they had to look for work, having been promoted through the organization without having to resubmit formal details.

☛ **Interview advice and practice.** The considerations about CVs, above, apply again here. The thought of an interview can be terrifying for many and so a little practice and feedback can prove to be of great benefit.

☛ **Advice on employment elsewhere.** The better outplacement consultants will have considerable knowledge, both local and national, about who is recruiting and the types of jobs on offer. They often send out a 'blanket fax' to suitable companies notifying them of the redundancy exercise and listing the job types available. They may then also take care of forwarding CVs to interested parties. Some consultants act as headhunters and so will have a network of existing clients.

☛ **Skills analysis.** This involves analysing and packaging the qualifications and experience of each person into 'marketable chunks'. People who have been out of the job market for a while tend to undersell themselves, underestimating the marketability of their skills and experience.

☛ **Advice on 'non-standard' working.** Getting back to our 'flexible firm' model, other opportunities increasingly exist in the jobs market, from part-time work to freelancing and self-employment. As well as direct advice, the consultant will be able to put people in touch with useful bodies, from government departments to Chambers of Commerce and professional societies.

☛ **Retraining.** Although the outplacement consultants are unlikely to train people themselves, they will advise on potential training on offer, relevant providers and sources of finance. This will often follow the skills analysis. It could well be that if only a small skills gap is identified between taking the person from being 'quite desirable' to 'highly desirable' in the jobs market, it may only require a short period of training to fill the gap.

07-5

☛ **Arranging interviews and negotiating salary.** This is an extension of the headhunting activity and will normally only apply to senior staff. The consultant will make the initial introduction, answer initial queries on the candidate's behalf, arrange the interview(s) and act as the intermediary in agreeing a salary. Headhunters are normally less diffident about asking for a higher salary than candidates — particularly those who are being made redundant. To give balance to this, they will normally advise candidates if they are pricing themselves out of the market.

Elitist Practices?

It is not uncommon for organizations to offer a 'tiered' system of outplacement benefits to redundant staff, based on seniority. Is this fair? It might work on the following hypothetical basis:

- ☞ **Clerical and admin staff:** Help in CV preparation and information on organizations in the local area currently recruiting.

- ☞ **Management and professional grades:** Help in CV preparation, forwarding CV to local and national organizations, and interview practice.

- ☞ **Senior managers and directors:** Skills analysis, CV preparation, interview practice, forwarding CV to local/national organizations and subsequent salary negotiation.

For: It can be argued that more senior staff will find it harder to get new jobs, simply because they are nearer the top of the 'jobs pyramid' where fewer suitable positions are available — so they need more help. In addition, the shock of redundancy may be greater after they have spent so much time building up a successful career. Finally, to obtain a comparable position, they are more likely than junior staff to have to relocate.

Any room out there for one from senior management?

Against: The shock of redundancy may be just as great for lower levels of staff. It may be even greater if they have few savings and if they are in an area of already high unemployment. The senior staff will have been paid far more and should have been able to build-up a financial 'buffer' against such an occurrence. And didn't they get the organization into this mess in the first place?

ACTIVITY 8

There are some other basic forms of help which organizations can offer either instead of, or in addition to, outplacement consultants, when helping staff to find jobs with other organizations. What types of support are you aware of?

Compare your notes against ours in Appendix 1.

07-5

The 'Resource Centre' Development

Not everyone wants to be 'spoon-fed' by an outplacement organization or take advantage of the full range of help available. They may wish to 'dip in' to what is on offer when it suits them. Similarly, the organization itself may not, for operational reasons, want large groups of staff attending workshops *en masse.*

A way around this is to set-up a Resource Centre. This will normally be run by the outplacement consultants and will contain literature on training opportunities, adverts and information from other organizations and application resources (paper, stamps, etc.). One or more members of the consultancy will be present to give advice when requested. Generally, these are located within the organization, space permitting. Employees are able to visit the centre as and when it suits them, perhaps at lunchtime or at the end of the day. Alternatively, the organization may designate certain times for people from different departments to attend.

This option is of particular use if there is a long lead-in time to the redundancies — perhaps if the organization is relocating to another area in, say, 6 to 12 months' time.

Some people will undoubtedly take longer than others to find new jobs. The organization may therefore arrange for them to receive advice on the benefits available to them. Similarly, those receiving substantial lump sum redundancy payments may be offered investment advice, again paid for by the organization.

07-5-2   Redeployment

An alternative to moving people out altogether is to move them to other parts of the organization. How this happens in practice will depend on the number of people involved and the overall size and structure of the organization. For example:

☞	If only one or two people are being made redundant, there is a much greater possibility of moving them to other positions than if a large group is affected. The bigger the organization, the easier this will normally be.

☞	If the organization has several sites and is closing down one, or part of one, the possibility exists for people to be transferred to another site (the practicalities of this are discussed in Section 07-5-3, 'Resettlement').

'Downshifting'

This term arose at the end of the 'lunch is for wimps' 1980s. After a decade in which everyone was expected to be an entrepreneur and work, work, work, some people decided to take an alternative route. They decided to take a cut in pay and do something they felt was personally more rewarding — perhaps allowing them to work from home or spend more time with their loved ones. Over time they may have built up reasonable savings, or perhaps they had paid off the mortgage, or got the kids off their hands. Whatever the scenario, they decided to bail out of the regimented career path expected of them.

So what? Well the point is that we need to consider each 'worker' as an individual. We live in a pluralist society in which people have a multiplicity of interests and aspirations, often removed from the 'I joined the company at 16, worked my way up and retired at 65' stereotype. So when each person threatened with redundancy is advised and counselled, the enlightened HR practitioner or line manager needs to start with a blank sheet of paper. Don't assume that because Fred is a Management Accountant on £45,000 a year that he wants to move to a similar post and won't be happy with alternatives.

Fred may have a secret desire to move into sales or purchasing. He may be an avid gardener, who would be happy joining the company's grounds maintenance team, given the opportunity. Most people, in normal circumstances, do not actually pursue this type of change, usually because they fear a drop in income. But if the situation is forced, as with redundancy, they can have a less cautious attitude.

 PAUSE TO REFLECT

But haven't we, so far, assumed something here? Is redeployment in terms of redundancy merely a stage in the redundancy process?

Other life changes can occur which result in redeployment being considered. An employee may decide on a career change at any time — they may simply have become bored or fed up with what they are doing. It's at this time that the organization has to decide whether it wants to lose them, or if it will facilitate a change of direction.

07-5

If someone becomes disabled, whether through an accident or illness, they may simply not be able to perform their old role and will need to be redeployed elsewhere within the organization. The Disability Discrimination Act (1995) has increased the onus on employers in this respect. Companies employing 20 people or more must ensure that *employment practices and premises do not disadvantage someone with a disability.* This applies to recruitment, terms of employment, opportunities for promotion, other benefits and dismissal.

Redeployment, though, is not just about responses to negative issues, such as plant closures or changes at the individual level. An organization may be undergoing expansion, resulting in developments such as:

☛ A change in organizational structure
☛ The opening of a new part of the organization — perhaps a branch, depot or manufacturing plant
☛ A move overseas, as part of 'organic' growth or through merger or acquisition.

Strategic redeployment of this kind may lead to a range of possible scenarios for individuals within the business, including:

☞ *Permanent redeployment* to either a duplicate post, or a new, but related role. Such expansion provides promotional opportunities for staff which perhaps were not there previously. Organizations often prefer a 'safe pair of hands' in key roles within nascent business units.

☞ *Secondments* to new parts of the organization until they are established and operating to a satisfactory standard.

☞ A *training* or 'immersion' period prior to redeployment, particularly if this means moving abroad, with the demands of a new language and culture.

☞ *'Trailblazing'* staff may be used on a repeat basis to get new outlets up and running. Often experienced entrepreneurial employees, they are often involved in establishing new markets, and in recruiting and training new staff before moving on to the next 'greenfield' site.

Some large centralized organizations have a policy of seconding managers to head office to participate in strategic and business planning processes. The benefits are thought to be that planning is 'reality checked' by front-line managers, while secondees gain a deeper appreciation of central concerns and practices.

 ### 07-5-3 Resettlement

Resettlement follows on from redeployment and, in practice, 'dovetails' with it. Once redeployment has been agreed as a path to take, people have to be transferred to their new roles and/or new places of work. It is not just a physical move, it is a psychological one as well, so planning must again be thorough to avoid hiccups or accusations of callousness.

There is something of a continuum in terms of redeployment and the subsequent resettlement. Person A may simply have been redeployed to another team in the next office, essentially doing the same job. Person B may still be on the same site, but working in a totally new role. Person C may be transferring to a new site, 150 miles away. Clearly, we will not manage each resettlement in the same way.

ACTIVITY 9

Below are three brief descriptions of how three different people are being redeployed. What practical considerations would you consider and implement for each person? Consider their anxieties and how these might be addressed. Their transfer dates are three months away.

Person A. Name: Susan. Telesales Agent. Same job, although selling different products. Moving to a different team in the same office.

Person B. Name: Frank. From Accountant to Sales Rep. Same site, but entirely new job.

07-5

Person C. Name: Siobhan. Marketing Director. Moving 150 miles.

Compare your comments against our thoughts in Appendix 1.

Resettlement need not only apply to internal redeployment programmes. Some organizations, such as the British Army, take the view that there are benefits to be had from offering structured resettlement support to everyone who reaches the end of their contract of employment. In business terms, probably the main benefit is the impact on the morale of remaining employees.

CASE STUDY: SURVIVOR SYNDROME

'Survivor syndrome' has become a prominent concept in the theory of change management. Outlined by Dr Leon Deutsch (1997), after his pioneering work with survivors of the Holocaust, it identifies a condition affecting those who have managed to escape in a situation where others, perhaps people they knew, suffered loss. In the case of the Holocaust survivors, the loss they escaped was clearly of the worst kind, but the concept is now commonly applied to people who have survived in hostage situations, accidents and also large redundancy programmes. The survivors are said to experience feelings of guilt, apathy and bitterness towards those they identify as the perpetrators.

For organizations planning redundancies, resettlement is an important strategy to reduce the effects of 'survivor syndrome' among remaining employees.

By demonstrating a fair and caring approach to those leaving the organization, they benefit from the reciprocated trust and commitment of 'survivors'.

There are also 'macro' arguments for taking the ethical stance on resettlement. Consider a large manufacturer which is forced to make thousands redundant in certain of its plants. The consequences of not supporting resettlement might be dire:

☞ *For those leaving the organization*, low prospects of finding work, severely cut income, drastic alteration of lifestyle and perhaps social situation
☞ *For local businesses*, significant drop in demand for supplies and everyday products and service bought by the workforce
☞ *For local support agencies*, greater demand on training, employment and information services, consequent drain on public funding
☞ *For the organization*, bad publicity, loss of good will from the public and from government.

Of course, resettlement even of the most effective kind cannot solve all the employment and microeconomic problems caused by a large-scale redundancy, but it can help to reduce them significantly.

07-6 RECRUITMENT AND SELECTION TECHNIQUES

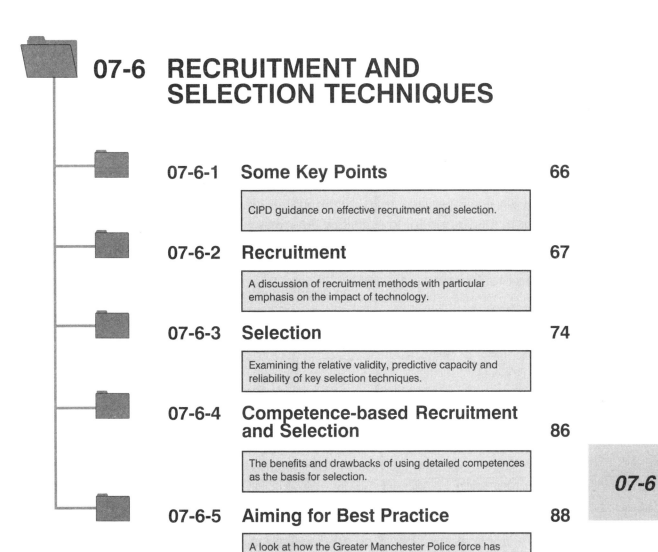

07-6-1 Some Key Points   66

CIPD guidance on effective recruitment and selection.

07-6-2 Recruitment   67

A discussion of recruitment methods with particular emphasis on the impact of technology.

07-6-3 Selection   74

Examining the relative validity, predictive capacity and reliability of key selection techniques.

07-6-4 Competence-based Recruitment and Selection   86

The benefits and drawbacks of using detailed competences as the basis for selection.

07-6-5 Aiming for Best Practice   88

A look at how the Greater Manchester Police force has upgraded its recruitment and selection process.

07-6

07-6 RECRUITMENT AND SELECTION TECHNIQUES

07-6-1 Some Key Points

Before we cover some of the traditional and newer methods of recruitment and selection, it is important to consider the overall approach adopted by the organization and the people it charges with carrying out these vital tasks. The UK's Chartered Institute of Personnel and Development (CIPD) (1997) has put forward the following key points:

☞ Organizations should have a recruitment and selection policy which is communicated to all staff

☞ Equality of opportunity should be an integral part of the recruitment process

☞ All recruitment systems must be fair, consistent and valid

☞ All selection tools must be validated

☞ Recruitment and selection must take into account the needs of the individual as well as the needs of the organization

☞ Advertisements must not make misleading claims, or present misleading information

☞ All personnel involved in the selection process must be trained to an acceptable standard for the tools they are using

☞ All applications should be acknowledged, if possible, and treated confidentially

☞ Recruitment advertisements should never contain age barriers or age-related criteria of any description.

We have already looked at job descriptions and person specifications in Section 07-3 of this dossier. We can now start the process of trying to employ the people we need.

PAUSE TO REFLECT

We often hear the term *'recruitment and selection'*, which tends to imply that it's one activity. But is it? Think about the distinction before reading further.

The essential difference is that *recruitment* is about attracting suitable candidates, whereas *selection* is the process of filtering the applicant pool to find the best candidate(s).

 07-6-2　Recruitment

It is often forgotten that a substantial part of a Human Resource practitioners' work is actually involved with sales and marketing in its broadest sense: for example, promoting new ideas, reward systems and structural changes to the existing workforce. On the resourcing side it means promoting the organization (to external candidates) and roles (to external and internal candidates).

There is an element of 'selling' on both sides — candidates are also promoting themselves to the organization. The proportion of selling between organization and candidate is a *dynamic* factor dependent upon the scarcity of skilled labour. For example, in recent years, the demand for Information Technology skills has rocketed. The best people have been able to pick and choose who they work for and have commanded large salaries. Since demand for labour in this sector has outstripped supply, the onus has been on organizations to attract staff, to the point where it is a matter of serious discussion whether the UK government should alter its immigration policies to attract more skilled IT workers.

07-6

 ACTIVITY 10

Think about the situation described above in the IT skills market. What potential impact do you think this could have on an organization? Think in terms of other staff and costs. Note down some conclusions here.

Now refer to our comments in Appendix 1.

As the feedback to the previous activity demonstrated, there are many ways of attracting the right staff. These include:

Printed media: ☞ Local newspapers (in some areas this may include regional business publications) ☞ National newspapers ☞ Professional and trade journals ☞ Other non-trade journals or magazines.	**Other media:** ☞ Radio — local or national ☞ Internet — again this can either be national or local (your regional newspaper group may, for example, have its own recruitment web site) ☞ Direct mail ☞ TV (including teletext) or cinema ☞ Billboards (including buses, etc.).
External organizations: ☞ Employment agencies ☞ Headhunters/consultants ☞ Job centres ☞ Outplacement consultants ☞ Armed forces resettlement organizations.	**Educational establishments:** ☞ Careers Advisors (this includes those within schools, colleges and universities) ☞ Careers fairs (including the traditional university 'milk round') ☞ Student societies ☞ College tutors.
Professional bodies: ☞ Trade associations/societies ☞ Chambers of Commerce ☞ Trade unions ☞ Industry networking.	**In-house methods:** ☞ Notice-board/posters ☞ Newsletters ☞ Email bulletin boards ☞ Open days ☞ Utilizing past applications (this is far easier if a computerized logging system is maintained) ☞ Cash incentives for existing employees to introduce a candidate to the organization.

Cost, time and resources will be essential determinants of which recruitment methods are used. But there are others. Line managers often put pressure on Human Resources staff to recruit people as quickly as possible to relieve operational pressures. In smaller organizations there may not be anyone who has the time to take care of the full recruitment process. This could mean, for example, that a recruitment agency is used instead of advertising directly. In this case there will be a trade-off between time and money.

Many organizations, particularly those which are large and diverse, use advertising agencies to handle their contact with various media. A significant cost is involved, but this can often be reduced by the preferential discounts the agencies are able to obtain (because they are dealing with the publications on a regular basis on behalf of a wide variety of clients).

The Internet

The biggest single innovation in advertising (together with the electronic receipt of applications) has, of course, been the advance of the Internet. Although still in its infancy, it is growing rapidly. During the year 1999/2000 the number of UK employers recruiting on the Internet doubled.

The Association of Graduate Recruiters states that around two-thirds of employers recruiting graduates now take online applications and almost nine out of ten students in their final year at university go online to look for work. Their report, 'Going to Work on the Web' found that some employers wanted to transfer their entire application process online, but were deterred from doing so because they feared breaching equal opportunities legislation.

'Online recruitment will grow by 1,600% over the next five years'

This is the conclusion of a 2000 Morgan Stanley Dean Witter survey. So can traditional methods survive in the face of this proliferation? At present, it seems that it is not the preferred medium for senior positions, not least because such candidates don't like being viewed as one of the crowd — they may prefer the ego boost of being headhunted. At present there is also a deal of concern about the confidentiality of personal data (such as a CV or job application) when transmitted over the Internet.

This will change shortly according to Tim Nicholson, chief executive of the Recruitment and Employment Confederation, who comments: 'Soon Internet advertising will be the norm. At senior levels it enables search and selection to be on a global scale. But the Internet is only a tool to bring people together more quickly. Ultimately you have to assess if a certain individual, whether clerk or chief executive is going to be suitable for a particular job and fit into the organization. The Internet may help you to reach that point more quickly or more cheaply, but the final recruitment stage is a human decision.'

07-6

A prime benefit of online recruitment is speed, with 'instant' access to job details for applicants (advert, plus as much supplementary online information as the organization wishes to provide, including 'hot' links to its home web page). Costs can also be a fraction of what would be charged by, say, a national broadsheet, but this will depend on the service provider and the level of sophistication built into their site.

An organization normally has a choice of two Internet routes:

(1) Using their own web sites (according to the CIPD over 60% of Internet recruiters do this). This requires both technical expertise and the ability to handle what could potentially be large volumes of applications.

(2) Job boards, provided by third parties, many of which are now regular TV advertisers. Some of these market themselves as 'career management sites', giving advice on CV preparation or using psychometric exercises. The Recruitment and Employment Federation calculates that there are currently around 5,000.

CASE STUDY:
ASDA

In 2000, the UK retailer ASDA expected to recruit 65 graduates, with the Internet being a prime tool. It was, in fact, one of the first companies to recruit graduates by this method. Its humorous approach promises 'scenes of nudity, immense challenges and early responsibility which some people may find disturbing'. ASDA's web site includes pages entitled 'In the raw' and 'Leaving nothing to the imagination'. Candidates are also invited to request a video called 'The Naked Truth'. And any applicants who fail their filter quiz are redirected to the Sainsbury's web site!

Graduate Resourcing Manager Andrea Vowles (2000) regards targeting the right audience as imperative:

> *'The web site must be designed to be interesting and fun to read. We make the process interactive by including a quiz and video, but the most important rule is to have a simple application process. On some company web sites it takes 45 minutes to complete the application and no one can be bothered with that'.*

Job Boards Already Dead?

It is said that online recruitment web sites already face a bleak future, even though they have been with us for a relatively short time. The new kid on the block is the *Internet Directory*, which gives access to every job on the Internet, giving candidates access to any positions that match their chosen criteria. The managing director of Alljobs, Stephen O'Donnell, who has launched such a directory (Sourceuk.com), says that:

> *'Recruitment web sites are a middleman too far. They can't possibly provide the added value of a consultancy. Within a year, all serious recruiters and most major employers will have their own site, and our directory will enable candidates to access all the relevant jobs. Job boards will be redundant.'*

The benefits of technology developments for selection and recruitment in enlightened organizations can be enormous. Cisco says it has reduced the length of the recruitment cycle by two-thirds, while ICL claim a twentyfold reduction in the cost of graduate recruitment.

Helen Vandevelde (2000) believes that along with the steep rise in numbers of self-employed people in Europe and the USA, developing recruitment technology is promoting more fluid contractual relationships. Talented people are stimulated by this, as they move from contract to contract, adding 'knowledge assets' with every new project they work on.

PAUSE TO REFLECT

What effect do you think these trends might have on the HR function?

Vandevelde foresees the following key developments:

- Contracts of employment will become more specific, with each party agreeing an explicit statement of what will be provided. Neither will expect anything more.

> *'The days of pretending that we trade job security for loyalty are numbered'.*

- Customized contracts will become the norm, with knowledge workers in particular choosing employers rather than vice versa.
- Employers will need to invest more heavily in their employees' future to retain them.
- Recruiting people will be less important than organizing them.

> *'There's a big difference between being a good employer and a good organizer. The organizer offers opportunities rather than jobs — spaces where creativity can flourish. The organizer takes an idea, identifies the resources required to realize it and then attracts those resources'.*

Vandevelde goes on to explain that what is starting to be mapped out is a more flexible employment model that incorporates such elements as:

- Instantly tapping a skilled resource pool
- Paying retainers in return for availability
- Sharing staff with competitors
- Forming alliances with networks of 'niche' knowledge workers
- Project contracting with individuals.

07-6

A Word on Application Forms . . .

Application forms are widely used as a means of obtaining initial candidate details. The benefit they have over a CV (*curriculum vitae*) (sometimes called a *résumé*) is that they force the candidate to give the precise information the organization wants, rather than what the candidate wishes to supply. If carefully designed, they can knock hours off the sifting process by ensuring that the candidate responds to questions directly related to the person specification or job description, in order of priority. A trained sifter will therefore be able to spend the minimum time on each application.

Application forms should:

☞ Be realistic and appropriate to the level of the job
☞ Be piloted for readability and ease of completion
☞ Not request personal information unless relevant to the job
☞ State the procedure for taking up references, how these will be used and at what stage in the recruitment process they will be taken
☞ Use clear language
☞ Be accompanied by details of the job and clear information about the application and selection procedure.

And on References . . .

References should be obtained to check factual information, such as qualifications. However, they should not ask former employers to supply subjective opinion as to an applicant's likely future performance. This type of data is unreliable and misleading.

Whenever a reference is given, the referee has a duty to both the subject and the recipient. Failure to perform these duties is considered either defamation or negligence under the law. The former is unlikely, since the defence of 'qualified privilege' applies if referees believe the statements they make (even though they may be prejudiced and have no basis in reality). However, negligence can easily be shown to occur, particularly if the employer issuing the reference has not taken the time to check the facts. Referees who are 'economical with the truth' should also be cautious, since even if the content of a statement is true, omissions can themselves constitute negligence. There is no duty to give a reference, however, so this may be regarded as enough to confirm the bare employment details.

And on Medical Examinations . . .

☞ It is reasonable to require the completion of a health questionnaire where good health is relevant to the job

☞ Any particular physical and/or medical requirement should be made clear in the job advertisement or other recruitment literature

☞ When it is necessary for medical records to be obtained, the requirements of the Medical Reports Act 1998 must be observed (gaining the applicant's consent)

☞ Organizations should pay for medical examinations when required.

CASE STUDY: TOYOTA

NEW

TON-UP TURBO

We mentioned recruitment at Toyota's Derby plant in Section 07-2-4 of this dossier. You will recall that they had over 35,000 applications for 3,000 jobs. So how did they handle them? Their systematic approach included the following key methods:

07-6

☞ They have a 'flat' structure, with only six job classifications.

☞ They do not have job descriptions. All employees are expected to do whatever they are trained for/capable of.

☞ They were less interested in the skills people already had, but rather in the type of person they would be. Ninety per cent of those recruited had never worked in the industry before.

☞ In tandem with a management consultancy they wrote *recruitment dimensions* for every job classification — i.e. required behaviour and how to measure it. This took several months and covered, for example, oral communication, problem identification, problem solving, teamwork, initiative, adaptability, motivation and work tempo. They looked for a desire to develop and learn new skills.

☞ At their assessment centres, applicants were given an introduction to the company, including a video showing exactly what it is like to work in a car plant.

☞ The assessment exercises included a numerical test and a job-fit questionnaire (written by the consultancy).

☞ All levels of staff went through the tests, which became progressively harder for higher level jobs.

☞ Examples of tests were sent to all candidates in advance, partly to circumvent any racial/cultural/language difficulties.

☞ The first stage of the process was completely automatic, with a computer scoring the tests and sending out rejection letters.

 ### 07-6-3 Selection

Think about the times you've applied for jobs. What key stages were involved? They were probably virtually the same as the procedures encountered by most of the people you know.

It's probable that you would have completed an *application form*, attended at least one *interview* and then received a *formal offer*, subject to satisfactory references. This has been described as *'the classic trio'* (Mark Cook, 1993).

This approach is still taken by most organizations today. However, the research undertaken seems to show beyond doubt that other methods of selection have far greater predictive results. As far back as 1986, Robertson and Makin, reporting on selection techniques, concluded that *'the frequency of a method's use is inversely related to its known validity'*.

Research Results

The chart on the next page summarizes the thrust of recent research into the reliability of selection methods. It shows that traditional methods, such as interviews, are much poorer at predicting performance than more sophisticated techniques such as assessment centres and personality tests.

1.0	Perfect prediction
0.9	
0.8	
0.7	
	Assessment centres (promotion)
0.6	
	Work sample tests/ Ability tests
0.5	
	Assessment centres (performance)/ Personality tests (combination)
0.4	
	Biodata/ Structured interviews
0.3	
0.2	
	Typical interviews/ References
0.1	
0.0	
	Astrology/ Graphology/ Chance prediction
–0.1	

07-6

PAUSE TO REFLECT

Which of these methods have you experienced (either as selector or as candidate)? Which were most effective in your view?

It is worth pointing out here that, at a practical level, the 'classic trio' is normally the quickest and cheapest method and will no doubt still be the prime choice in 20 years' time.

Let's look at some of the methods.

(1)   Interviews

We'll give quite a lot of space to these, because of their continued dominance and their many pitfalls.

The so-called 'halo effect' has been known for many years in connection with interviews. Essentially it states that interviewers make up their mind about candidates in the first couple of minutes of meeting them. Subsidiary questions they ask are used to substantiate the opinions they have already formed.

At the beginning of 2000 the American Psychological Society again revealed that most interviewers decide within a minute whether someone is suitable for the job.

The following comments, by Andrew Swift (2000) of the recruitment consultants Price Jamieson, make interesting reading:

> *'Personality is becoming increasingly important. There's a chronic skills shortage in such areas as new media, so companies are looking at who will fit in with their culture, rather than who has experience. Technology is changing so fast anyway that there's no point recruiting people who have today's skills. What we need are people with creative, dynamic personalities who are not afraid to push into the unknown. Traditional interview rules are all well and good, but when people need staff in a hurry they learn the benefits of intuition.'*

Psychologist Ros Taylor (2000), having interviewed the chief executives of 80 blue-chip companies, reported:

> *'Really, to make a good impression, you don't even get time to open your mouth. An interviewer's response to you will generally be preverbal. How you walk through the door, what your posture is like, whether you smile, whether you have a captivating aura, whether you have a firm, confident handshake. You've got about half a minute to make an impact and after that all you are doing is building on a good or bad first impression . . . it is a very emotional response'.*

Occupational psychologist Ben Williams (2000) doesn't even agree that candidates have the luxury of 30 seconds:

> *'I'd argue it's more like a third of a second, which is basic human reaction time. In that time, like animals, we make a judgement based on whether there is a perceived threat, in which case our instinct is to run, or a favourable response, when we feel it's safe to approach. Everything that happens after, only backs that up.'*

I'm 'ere for the interview - ain't I!

Psychologists call the tendency to fixate on character traits the 'Fundamental Attribution Error'— that the way a person will behave in an interview situation reflects the way that person will always behave. In other words, we don't need to know someone in order to believe that we do know them.

CASE STUDY: HELL AND HUMAN RESOURCES

A Human Resources officer got a call from Satan — would she like to work in Hell? She went down for a meeting and loved what she saw — wild partying and champagne flowing. 'Great, when can I start?' she said. The following Monday morning she reported for work. But Hell was a very different place. There was no partying and everyone was very depressed. 'What's happened? Things have changed so much from when I was last here'. 'Oh that', said Satan laughing, 'that was just the job interview — you're an employee now.'

The traditional interview is one that is relatively unstructured, asking almost random questions. Anderson and Shackleton's 1993 review gave the following classifications for traditional interviews having low predictive results:

07-6

☞ *The expectancy effect.* Too much influence being given to positive or negative expectations of a candidate formed from the CV/application form.

☞ *The self-fulfilling prophecy effect.* Questions being asked to confirm initial impressions gained before the interview or in its early stages.

☞ *The primacy effect.* Too much emphasis being placed on impressions gained and information gathered early in the interview.

☞ *The stereotyping effect.* Assuming that particular characteristics are typical of members of a particular group.

☞ *The prototyping effect.* Interviewers favouring or seeking out a particular type of personality, regardless of job-related factors.

☞ *The halo and horns effect.* Interviewers rating candidates as good or bad across the board and so reaching unbalanced decisions.

☞ *The contrast effect.* Allowing the experience of interviewing one candidate to affect the way other candidates are interviewed later in the process.

☞ *Negative information bias effects.* Giving more weight to perceived negative points about candidates than to those that are more positive.

☞ *The similar-to-me effect.* Giving preference to candidates seen as having a similar background or personality.

☞ *The personal liking effect.* Interviewers basing decisions on whether or not they personally like or dislike the candidate.

☞ *The information overload effect.* Judgements being made based on only a small amount of the information provided.

☞ *The fundamental attribution error effect*. Incorrectly assuming that some action on the part of the candidate was caused by their personality, rather than a simple response to events.

☞ *The temporal extension effect*. Assuming that a candidate's behaviour at interview, such as nervousness, is typical of their general demeanour.

PAUSE TO REFLECT

Have you been guilty of any of the above — either in interviews or when meeting people for the first time?

(a) Panel or one-to-one?

At least some of the subjective problems listed above can be reduced by having more than one person interviewing the candidate at the same time. One of the positive things about one-to-one interviews is that they enable interviewers to put candidates at ease and establish rapport very quickly. However, it is quite difficult to do this while at the same time trying to follow up with objective, probing questions. Panel interviews of several people should eliminate personal bias altogether (unless there is one very dominant member). The drawback of large panels, though, is that they can provide a very artificial environment, can be nerve-racking for already nervous candidates and can also be badly managed. So-called 'sequential' interviews, when candidates are interviewed by several people consecutively, may again help to reduce personal bias, but again need to be managed very carefully to avoid duplication and time wasting. It becomes very boring for the candidate to be asked the same questions by different people and gives a negative impression.

At this stage it is easy to see that a great deal of thought needs to go into the interview process — both in terms of desired input and desired output. It is probably best to start out with a blank piece of paper when designing the programme for each vacancy or set of vacancies.

(b) Structured interviews

You will have noted from the earlier chart that structured interviews have a higher predictive value than traditional non-structured interviews.

Structured interviews have the following features:

- ☛ Careful planning of questions takes place before the interviews
- ☛ All candidates are asked the same questions
- ☛ Answers are scored against a previously agreed rating scale
- ☛ Questions are based on the skills and behaviour needed to be successful in the job.

 ACTIVITY 11

What is the main disadvantage of a structured approach to interviews? Put yourself in the candidate's chair.

Now refer to our comments in Appendix 1.

Semi-structured interviews, as their name suggests, are not as rigid. They target a number of topic areas for discussion, but allow more spontaneity, with follow-up questions to the answers given by candidates. As a result, there is a greater two-way exchange. *Multiple approaches* essentially include both structured questions and informality; at the beginning of the interview structured questions are avoided, in order to relax the candidate and allow him/her to open up. Structured questions are introduced later, followed by informality at the end to leave the candidate feeling relaxed again and that his interviewer is 'human'.

07-6

(2) Additional Selection Techniques

Although most organizations still use interviews, these are now often enhanced by additional selection tools. They normally add to the cost (not least in time) of the selection process, but have been shown to substantially increase the likelihood of choosing the right people — which is in the interests of *both* the organization and the individual. Let's look at some of them.

(a) Ability tests

The evidence is that around 75% of employers now use some sort of ability test(s), although they are mainly used as a back-up for other selection methods.

They can essentially be divided into two groups:

(i)   Specific job-related tests (a classic example being typing tests).

(ii)   General tests of mental ability. (Often these are tests of literacy or numeracy and tend to be used to weed out less able candidates, rather than being a prime factor in who is appointed. However, a recruiter with a personal bias can blow up a good score out of all proportion, or disregard a poor score as irrelevant or a one-off.)

A major point to be made about job-related tests is that it is no use giving one to someone who has not done that particular type of work. A skilled typist should be expected to perform well, but someone who has never used a typewriter will obviously fare disastrously. It does not, though, mean they cannot become a skilled typist. In these type of situations it is possible to devise 'trainability tests' — that is, tests which show how quickly and to what anticipated level a person can be trained to do the required job.

Research has shown the validity of mental ability testing, but the main argument is whether a relatively short pencil and paper type test can be effective, or whether a much longer battery of tests is required. A major plus factor is that they do not have to be redesigned for new jobs. Computerization has brought further benefits, taking candidates' tests and providing automatic scoring.

Many tests are based on a so-called 'control population'. The manufacturers try out the tests on hundreds, if not thousands of volunteers to establish performance criteria against which subsequent people are judged (i.e. they may score better than, say, 90% of the control population). There may be specific control populations for comparison, such as managers or graduates.

 ACTVITY 12

Mental ability tests tend to be purchased from external suppliers, rather than being designed by individual organizations for their own use. What is the practical problem here?

Now compare your notes against our comments in Appendix 1.

(b)   Personality (psychometric) tests

Before progressing further, it is worth noting the Chartered Institute of Personnel and Development's guidance on psychological tests, which include measures of personality. These are:

☞   Everyone responsible for the application of tests, including evaluations, interpretation and feedback, should be trained to at least the level of competence recommended by the British Psychological Society.

☞   Potential test users should satisfy themselves that it is appropriate to use tests at all before incorporating tests into their decision-making processes.

☞   Users should satisfy themselves that any tests they decide to use actually measure factors which are relevant to the employment situation.

☞   Users must satisfy themselves that all tests they use have been rigorously developed and that claims about their validity and effectiveness are supported by statistical evidence.

☞   Care must be taken to ensure equality of opportunity among all those individuals required to take tests.

☞   The results of single tests should not be used as the sole basis of decision-making. This is particularly relevant with regard to personality tests.

There is, and has been for many years, much debate about the use of personality tests and their validity. As with ability tests, they have usually been based around answers to questionnaires. Many now have software applications, which are able to generate substantial written reports from questionnaires which may take as little as ten minutes to complete. They tend to be used for certain categories of staff, rather than the whole workforce (e.g. managers, graduates). In contrast, ability tests tend to have a much wider spread.

07-6

The validity of these tests is based on a number of critical assumptions:

☞   Human personality is measurable
☞   Human personality is stable over time
☞   Jobs can be analysed to determine the personality traits most suited to perform them successfully
☞   A questionnaire taking 30 to 60 minutes gives sufficient information about someone's personality to be of use in determining their suitability for a job.

Cooper and Robinson (1995) state that it is now possible to describe five basic psychological constructs (better known as 'traits') which explain the difference between individuals:

- ☞ *Extroversion – introversion*. The extent to which we enjoy excitement, socializing with others, and change.
- ☞ *Emotional stability*. How much we exhibit tension and anxiety.
- ☞ *Agreeableness*. The extent to which we avoid conflict and exhibit compassion.
- ☞ *Conscientiousness*. How well organized we are and how concerned we are at meeting deadlines and implementing plans.
- ☞ *Openness to experience*. How imaginative we are and how open we are to new experiences.

Some systems currently on the market also allow a profile to be drawn-up for the job (which can best be described as the psychological equivalent of a job description). It is then possible, by graph or computer-aided comparisons, to establish the 'fit' between candidate and job.

Slightly over-anxious response to a questionnaire!

(c) Biodata (biographical data)

Although around for a very long time, this method has only had a minority following in the UK (around 5% of employers). The reasons? It is surrounded by controversy and is expensive to develop. However, it is a technique with very good predictive ability.

With biodata, detailed information on an applicant's past is used to predict their likely future performance in a job.

The employer normally requires applicants to complete a comprehensive questionnaire about both their work and personal lives. The information tends to be in the form of multiple-choice questions, with the answers being fed into a computer to generate a score. This is compared against ratings of existing top-performing employees. Such questionnaires are designed for individual job types. As a very basic example, after researching a range of employees in a particular job type, if it is found that the top performing employees had an 'A' level in maths, then a question to this effect would be included in the questionnaire. If a maths 'A' level was not shown to be statistically relevant, a question would not be included.

There have been various criticisms of biodata:

☛ Candidates can feel unfairly treated, perhaps being rejected on one point (e.g. if they didn't attend a preferred university) after spending considerable time putting together their application and researching the organization concerned.
☛ It can therefore give the organization negative PR in the labour market.
☛ It is not transferable between different job groups.
☛ It needs to be based on a large sample group to be effective.
☛ It needs to be updated on a regular basis to maintain its appropriateness.
☛ It could potentially be illegal, if it discriminates against certain groups on grounds of race, sex or disability. Organizations must be very careful to ensure they do not contravene employment legislation.

07-6

 **ACTIVITY 13**

Discrimination in employment terms, relating to (for example) who is employed, promoted or made redundant, falls into two areas:

(1) *Direct* discrimination, and
(2) *Indirect* discrimination.

Find out what the difference is, either from your HR department, or from an employment law textbook. Note down your findings here and also how they might relate to biodata questionnaires.

Now read on.

Discrimination in employment terms, relating to who is employed, promoted or made redundant, falls into two areas:

Direct discrimination	Indirect discrimination
This is the most obvious form, perhaps when the employer tries only to recruit people of a certain sex or race. This is sometimes exacerbated by cultural norms (the vast majority of secretaries are female; we have traditionally had dinner ladies and paper boys).	This is less obvious, but its impact may be just as insidious in the way it disadvantages a particular part of society.

A recent example relates to alleged discrimination against female surgeons. It has been said that a disproportionate amount of female surgeons have been suspended after complaints of clinical incompetence from male colleagues. It seems that over the last 14 years, no female surgeon who has been suspended has been found guilty of wrongdoing or malpractice. However, only one actually got her job back after suspension.

Women comprise less than 5% of surgeons working in the UK, even though 54% of medical students are female. Flexible training and working, essential for women with or starting families, seems very difficult and is viewed as second best. A 1998 BMA survey of flexible trainee surgeons indicated that colleagues were not perceived to be 'pulling their weight' unless they worked the very long hours seen as the norm in the medical profession.

(d) Assessment centres

You will recall from the earlier chart that assessment centres have been found to have very good predictive ability in choosing people who will perform well in their roles. It also seems to be a method preferred by many candidates ('enjoyed' would perhaps be too strong a word!). Again, a prohibiting factor is cost and so assessment centres tend to be used primarily by large organizations.

The typical centre involves bringing together several applicants for the same post and putting them through a variety of exercises, probably including one or more interviews. It could involve several of the selection techniques we have covered over one or more days and it is this breadth which seems to provide the high degree of success.

A typical assessment centre day for potential management trainees might look something like the following:

```
9.00 a.m. Reception/coffee

9.30       Organization's presentation, giving information about
           current structure, prospects and the day-to-day
           activities of management trainees. This could involve
           existing trainees.

10.30      Group exercise to evaluate aspects such as leadership
           and teamwork.

11.30      Individual presentations on a nominated subject.

12.30      Personality profile (individual).

1.30       Lunch.

2.30       Mathematical reasoning test.

3.30       Verbal reasoning test.

4.30       Individual (panel) interviews.  Some questions would be
           predetermined and the same for all candidates.  Others
           would be based on the earlier group exercise and
           individual presentation.  If possible, a copy of the
           personality profile report would have been given to
           each candidate prior to interview and some questions
           would be related to this (giving candidates the chance
           to comment on the report's accuracy).

6.00       Debrief, and confirmation of the next stage of the
           process.

6.15       Close.
```

07-6

Some organizations may reject candidates part-way through the day — for example if they need them to reach a certain score in one or more tests. Some organizations may inform candidates at the end of the day whom they have decided to appoint, or which candidates will go forward to the next stage (if there is one).

The above programme is for people who are unlikely to have had much work experience and so the exercises may be fairly general in their nature. For positions requiring more experience and professional/technical expertise, the activities will be more specific. The aim is to observe behaviour in job-related situations.

07-6-4   Competence-based Recruitment and Selection

Much time, effort and money has been spent by some organizations on developing competence frameworks. They often underpin the whole HR function, offering such benefits as:

☞   Streamlining and standardizing processes
☞   Ensuring equality in the treatment of staff
☞   Helping to define what is acceptable behaviour.

A competence is a list of behaviour descriptions defining how an individual operates in a particular field. Specifying the abilities required to do a job has long been seen as the first stage in effective selection. Tony Keenan, Professor of Human Resource Management at Heriot-Watt University, states (2000):

'The appearance of behavioural competencies has led to much clearer specifications of performance requirements. There seems little doubt that competencies, being based on observable behaviours, offer a sounder foundation for selection than previous approaches — providing that the techniques used to generate and apply competencies are sound.'

Keenan identifies several distinct approaches to competences, with each one being developed for a different purpose:

☞   Those based on the Management Charter Initiative stress minimum standards and are particularly useful for training & development.
☞   So-called McBer behavioural competences are relevant for selection, because they emphasize excellence.
☞   Organizational competences take a broader approach, reflecting what the organization as a whole is competent to do.

His survey results indicate an increasing uptake of competences, but found that few HR practitioners were aware that different approaches existed, or which approach was adopted in their own organizations.

The Pearn Kandola occupational psychology consultancy regards recruitment and performance management processes that rely exclusively on competences as flawed. For example, utilizing competences for the recruitment of graduates will identify those candidates who can demonstrate behaviours relevant to an organization's needs, but will not predict their success in the job or how long they will stay.

The Pearn Kandola consultancy explains (2000):

'The context of the selection process is different from that of the job. In job simulation exercises, applicants are given the chance to show some aspects of their performance without the full context of the job, such as relationships with colleagues, communication methods and resources. But there is no guarantee that the candidate will produce all of the same behaviours in the workplace. In many selection processes, the assessment focuses on how an applicant behaves during an exercise. Little attention is paid to whether they actually complete the task successfully.'

They also criticize the 'cloning' tendency of competence frameworks:

'By focusing selection exclusively on the large number of behaviours found in many competence frameworks, an organization will employ people who all behave in the same way. This method ignores those who may have a different approach to a problem, but who are still effective workers and could prove to be important innovators and entrepreneurs for the organization.'

A read through of a selection of adverts for graduates will quickly reveal the same sort of attributes being requested by each organization, often covering the vague traits mentioned earlier. Essentially, they provide no reason why graduates should apply to one employer as opposed to another — they underline the similarities, rather than the differences.

07-6

One approach taken with clients is to narrow down the competences used in selection, which can perhaps reduce the number from 12 to 5. These are the ones the candidates definitely must have to be successful within the organization and they are identified in realistic situations. Applicants therefore get a very clear idea of the working environment, resulting in a lower dropout rate. Cutting down on the number of competences also enables greater diversity as it allows for wider differences between candidates.

Pearn Kandola concludes:

'Employers need to identify the full range of factors affecting performance. Only then will they be able to keep competencies in their rightful place: alongside other indicators of successful recruitment and performance management.'

Chartered psychologist Karen Moloney (Moloney and Gealy HR consultancy) has also pointed out that it may be discriminatory to reinforce competences that have led to success in the past. Bearing in mind that most senior (i.e. successful) people in organizations in the past were male, a competence framework based on their behaviours might result in indirect discrimination.

Karen Moloney warns:

> *'Research into the differences in male and female styles of managing suggests that the behavioural repertoires of male and female managers may be different. If the only successful managers you interview are male, then your competence framework might make it difficult for women to comply. Furthermore, the behavioural event methodology requires the interviewees to describe strategies they have undertaken that were particularly successful. Even if organizations include women in the cohort of effective managers interviewed, research suggests that those women will be more self-critical than men, disclose more negative evidence and find it harder to think of their successful strategies'.*

 ## 07-6-5   Aiming for Best Practice

For many organizations, particularly in the public sector, effective recruitment and selection is not just a matter of finding the best people — image and accountability are also important. The Police Force is perhaps the salient example of an organization which needs to get it right and be seen to get it right.

Greater Manchester Police employs around 7,000 officers and 3,300 support staff. There are also 700 special constables. GMP has an established policy of encouraging the recruitment of ethnic minority candidates.

Recruitment campaigns run throughout the year and at least one is specifically aimed at ethnic minority candidates. Each year around 3,500 applications for 450 officer positions are made, with approximately 200 from ethnic minorities. A range of methods is used to distribute information on police careers, including:

- Local press — adverts are placed in free-distribution newspapers and in specific publications such as *Eastern Eye* and the *AfroCaribbean Times*
- Leaflets — to homes in particular areas and through contact with religious leaders
- Television and radio appearances on AsianNet and Radio Piccadilly
- Multilanguage posters in a variety of outlets, including video shops and health centres
- Attendance at sporting events with confirmed high ethnic minority participation or followings, such as cricket and basketball
- Adverts on public transport, including buses and trams.

Open days have been held at a variety of locations, providing an opportunity for anyone interested to talk to officers and past trainees.

There are seven stages in the GMP selection process which, in total, can take several months.

(1)   Application forms. Standard application forms are obtained by attending an open day/evening or by post from Force headquarters. The forms are part of a comprehensive information pack, including a security questionnaire, a self-assessment questionnaire, and details of the selection process including timetable, equal opportunities policy and a variety of checklists.

Self-assessment is a pivotal part of the process. Accompanying the questionnaire is a self-assessment booklet, 'Is the job for me?' It is a self-selection tool containing 47 questions which cover desired character traits: communication with others, investigation, problem-solving and attitudes to practical issues such as shiftwork and acting as the face of authority. The booklet has been approved by the Equal Opportunities Commission.

(2)   Preliminary medical check. A height/weight, eyesight and colour vision check is taken before candidates can progress any further.

(3)   Entrance tests. The PIR is a Home Office test used nationally by all police forces. It measures 36 competences which have been produced by the Home Office's internal occupational psychology unit. The PIR comprises five separately timed sub-tests used to measure:

07-6

- ☞   Spelling and sentence construction
- ☞   Numerical problem solving
- ☞   Rapid and accurate checking of information
- ☞   Logical reasoning when given facts about events
- ☞   Careful observation and accurate recall of details.

The first four abilities are tested using pencil and paper under strict time limits (practice questions are available with the information pack). Observation skills are tested by means of a video showing a simulated crime scene. Candidates are not allowed to take notes and must answer a questionnaire requiring recall of the details they have viewed.

Successful candidates progress to the next stage, physical fitness. Those candidates who are not successful cannot reapply for 6 months. They are provided with tips on how to handle the range of exercises next time, rather than specific feedback on their performance.

(4)   Background enquiries. Prior to testing, background enquiries, including employer and academic reference, are made. Candidates not passing this, or any subsequent stage, cannot reapply for 12 months.

(5)   Physical tests. These are taken at the Force Training School, involving one minute each of sit-ups, press-ups, 'burpees' (a combination of a squat and a press-up) and a timed run. Candidates are informed of the physical benchmarks at an early stage, so there are few failures here.

(6)   Assessment centre. This is managed by a qualified occupational psychologist within the Personnel function and is also held at the Force Training School. It takes a full day and assessors are serving officers who perform the role of 'tutor constables' to new recruits. There are a total of 8 tests. These include:

☛   Assessing how candidates deal with aggression via role play
☛   Coping and problem solving skills
☛   A written test, which is a short essay on a current police issue (writing is still important for police officers)
☛   A group discussion to examine how candidates interact and to demonstrate communication skills.

(7)   Final interview. Candidates who get through the assessment centre then attend a structured interview that is also competence-based. This lasts about 35 minutes and is conducted jointly by an experienced officer and an experienced recruiter. Any areas of apparent weakness identified in the assessment centre are probed further, since candidates must pass in all competences.

Interviewers make their decisions straight after the interviews and candidates are immediately given feedback. Around eight interviews are conducted each day, with a pass rate of approximately 60%.

For successful candidates an offer of employment is made subject to a full medical. For those unsuccessful there are three possible outcomes:

☛   The candidate is unsuitable.
☛   They may have some development needs and would benefit from some time as a special constable.
☛   They are advised to reapply in 12 months, having addressed various developmental needs.

07-7 REWARDS

07-7-1 **An Overview** 92

> The part played by an effective reward system in HR strategy, and hence in overall business strategy, is often underestimated.

07-7-2 **The Building Blocks** 94

> Basic pay; contingent pay; allowances; benefits.

07-7-3 **Current Approaches to Rewards** 100

> How rewards have been redefined to prefer individual contributions over status.

07-7-4 **Prevailing Reward Structures** 102

> Seven ways organizations can structure and manage their pay systems.

07-7-5 **Incentives and Bonuses** 107

> The pros and cons of performance incentives at work.

07-7-6 **Performance Management** 110

> Reward is just one of several factors contributing to effective performance – here we look at the importance of aligning all of those factors.

07-7-7 **Measures to Retain Staff** 112

> How line managers and HR specialists can work together to retain talent.

07-7

07- 7 REWARDS

 ### 07-7-1   An Overview

Michael Armstrong (1996) encapsulates the concept of a reward system as follows:

> *'A reward system consists of an organization's integrated policies, processes and practices for rewarding its employees in accordance with their contribution, skill and competence and their market worth. It is developed within the framework of the organization's reward philosophy, strategies and policies, and contains arrangements in the form of processes, practices, structures and procedures which will provide and maintain appropriate types and levels of pay, benefits and other forms of reward.'*

 ## PAUSE TO REFLECT

The final few words of that paragraph are interesting. What do you think he's getting at?

We immediately tend to think of rewards as just being financial, but they also include non-financial rewards, such as:

☞ Recognition   ☞ Responsibility
☞ Praise   ☞ Personal growth.
☞ Achievement

To begin with, let's concentrate on the material side.

The key building blocks of a reward system are:

☞ *Processes* which measure the value of jobs, the contribution of individuals, and the range of employee benefits to be provided. These processes consist of job evaluation, market rate analyses and performance management.
☞ *Practices* for motivating people via financial and non-financial rewards.
☞ *Structures* to relate pay and benefit levels to the value of positions in the organization and to provide scope for rewarding people according to their performance, competence, skill and/or experience.

☞　*Schemes* providing financial rewards and incentives to people according to individual, group or organizational performance.

☞　*Procedures* for maintaining the system and for ensuring that it operates efficiently and flexibly, and provides value for money.

Any system must be fundamentally flexible to cope with changing times and circumstances. To quote Armstrong again:

> *'Employee reward is chiefly about process — ways of getting things done — rather than about rigid structures and sets of procedures.'*

That's the system and process, but what about strategy? Armstrong and Murlis (1991) state that reward strategies must:

☞　Be congruent with and support corporate values and beliefs

☞　Emanate from business strategies and goals

☞　Be linked to organizational performance

☞　Drive and support desired behaviour at all levels

☞　Fit the desired management style

☞　Provide the competitive edge needed to attract and retain the high level of skills the organization needs

☞　Be anchored to the realities of the labour market.

PAUSE TO REFLECT

The above points relate to what the organization needs, but what do you think employees want? What do *you* want?

07-7

Most people look for one or more of the following:

☞　The cliché of a 'fair day's work for a fair day's pay'

☞　A reward system which seems to allocate rewards fairly across the organization

☞　Some link between the individual's contribution to the organization and the rewards received

☞　Rewards consistent with those who are paid to do similar jobs in other organizations

☞　Some form of progression in pay — particularly in managerial and professional pay

☞　Certain minimum benefits — e.g. company sick pay and a pension scheme.

As long as the goals of the organization and the expectations of employees can be brought together, the reward strategy can be an extremely powerful tool in pushing forward the general HR strategy. It therefore occupies a pivotal place in Human Resource Planning. It can:

☞ Reinforce the aims and objectives of the organization, ensuring that employees' behaviour is directed at achieving them
☞ Give clear messages about the organization's culture and values, especially in terms of what behaviours are valued
☞ Assist in the motivation of employees
☞ Attract and retain good people
☞ Reward high performance ('high flyers') or specific project work
☞ Send out messages about unacceptable performance
☞ Establish priorities for individual post holders
☞ Encourage innovative and strategic thinking
☞ Encourage people to focus on those issues considered critical to organizational success
☞ Promote efficiency, effectiveness and high productivity.

 ## 07-7-2 The Building Blocks

What are the key building blocks of the reward process?

(1) Basic pay

This is the level of pay that constitutes the rate for the job. Although it is what the individual receives on a regular basis, regardless of performance, it may provide the basis for determining additional payments related to performance or skill. It may also affect pension and life assurance entitlement. The determinants of an individual's basic pay can be:

☞ Internal relativities — perhaps measured by a job evaluation system, placing it within a hierarchy (although the notion of a strict hierarchy is fast disappearing in the new process-based organizations).
☞ External relativities — that is, through rates being tracked in the local or national (or even international) markets.
☞ Individual negotiation.
☞ Negotiation via a trade union as part of the collective bargaining process.

Some organizations have pay rates or systems that have evolved over many years through individual managerial decisions or pressures from trade unions. They may have started from a sound premise, but have not been progressed on a systematic, planned basis. In short, they can be chaotic.

A WORD ON EQUAL PAY

As well as being out of date, the unplanned scenario above can be very unfair. Not only that, it may well be illegal. Equal pay legislation operates in the UK to ensure that the same rates of pay apply to jobs of equal worth. For a variety of reasons, often stemming from entrenched ideas about men being the family breadwinners, rates of pay for women in many sectors have lagged behind that of their male counterparts. The legislation was brought in to address this. A modern, systematic pay system should eradicate any such discrepancies and protect the organization against any claims of inequality being lodged with an Employment Tribunal.

The 1957 Treaty of Rome promoted 'the principle of equal pay for male and female workers for equal work, or work of equal value.' This was encapsulated within the UK's Equal Pay Act 1970, which ruled that employees performing the same roles, or roles which can be proved to be of equal effort and complexity, should receive the same rate of pay. As things stand at present, comparisons can only be made within the same organization, or between associated employers.

Basic pay may be expressed as an annual, weekly or hourly rate — sometimes referred to as a *time rate* system of payment. Although simple in theory, in practice this can be made more complicated by the addition of allowances, such as overtime and shift payments. Also, some systems may have *'spot rates'* — that is one rate for the job — while others may have a range of pay for each job grade, with progression taking place according to time in the job, competence or performance. For example, the historical pay system in local government for 'officer' grades has been based on an 'incremental' system. Job grades have been determined by job evaluation, with each grade having a number of increments (i.e. a salary ladder within the grade). Each year, subject to satisfactory performance, the employee moves up the ladder by one increment. An annual 'inflation-proofing' award has also been received.

07-7

(2)   Contingent pay

Rewards above basic pay may be given for such factors as performance, skill, competence or experience, and are known as 'contingent pay'. If they are not consolidated into basic pay they are referred to as 'variable pay'. They have been described as 'pay at risk' (i.e. it is not guaranteed — it may for example depend on how much someone sells).

The prime categories of contingent pay are:

- ☛ Individual performance-related pay (sometimes called merit pay).
- ☛ Bonuses — which are performance rewards paid as a lump sum. These may be individual or team related.
- ☛ Incentives — often used for sales people. These set targets and are meant to motivate employees.
- ☛ Commission — a special form of incentive in which sales people are paid a percentage of the sales value they achieve.
- ☛ Service-related pay — as per the local government example above.
- ☛ Competence-related pay — which varies depending on the individual's level of competence in the job.
- ☛ Contribution-related pay — this relates to both outputs (performance) and inputs (competence).
- ☛ Skill-based pay (sometimes referred to as knowledge-based pay) — which varies according to the level of skill attained.
- ☛ Career development pay — rewarding additional responsibilities as their careers develop laterally (a 'broad-banded' pay structure).

 PAUSE TO REFLECT

How does the pay system in your organization compare with the above? Does it contain more than one element? How would you like it to be constructed?

---

(3) Allowances

These are elements of pay provided as separate sums of money for things like:

- ☛ *Overtime.* Pay for overtime varies from 'time and a third' to 'time and a half' to 'double time' (the latter has traditionally been paid for weekend working, although this is being eroded as working on Saturday and Sundays is becoming commonplace in an increasingly secular society).
- ☛ *Stand-by payments.* When staff members have to stay at home in case they need to be called to work (the age of the mobile phone has given these people a great deal more freedom). Computer engineers are a classic example, waiting in case the dreaded 'crash' occurs.
- ☛ *Large city 'weighting'.* This primarily means London. The salary is topped-up in recognition of the higher costs of housing and transport (and to some extent just the sheer hassle of getting to work).

PAUSE TO REFLECT

Why is a London allowance paid as a lump sum? Why not just pay higher salaries?

There are three main reasons, all essentially financial:

☛ If the person obtained another position with the company outside London, the allowance could be removed. It would be much more difficult to do this if it were incorporated into basic pay.

☛ You will recall that basic pay is used for calculations for elements of contingent pay, such as bonuses. If the London weighting were incorporated into basic pay, the organization would have to pay out proportionately more. The same applies to annual negotiations on basic pay, i.e. allowances are negotiated separately.
NB: this would not apply to pensions (final salary), as calculations cover taxable earnings, and allowances are taxed at the going rate.

☛ *Car allowance*. Although cars are classified as benefits (see below), employees sometimes receive a lump sum payment if they choose to use their own vehicles.

☛ *Market subsidy*. Occasionally, particularly in the public sector, a lump sum payment has been paid on top of the job-evaluated grade, due to market scarcity. This currently often applies to IT staff, although in the mid-1980s it also applied to accountants.

07-7

(4) Employee Benefits

These are sometimes known as 'indirect pay' and include:

☛ Car
☛ Pension
☛ Medical insurance
☛ Personal accident insurance
☛ Permanent health insurance
☛ Death in service benefits
☛ Relocation expenses
☛ Annual leave (although legislation now gives minimum levels)
☛ Enhanced maternity leave
☛ Paternity leave
☛ Payment of telephone bills
☛ Payment of professional subscriptions
☛ Season ticket loans (travel, not football!)
☛ Long-service awards

☞ Subsidized catering
☞ Subsidized mortgage
☞ Sports and social facilities
☞ Sabbatical leave
☞ Time off for public duties.

This list is certainly not exhaustive. We will not discuss any of these individual items in depth, but there are a few issues to cover relating to benefits as a whole.

The mix and level of benefits will vary considerably between organizations, between industry sectors and between jobs. Subsidized mortgages are common in the financial services sector (simply because this sector supplies them), but not elsewhere. Although some people need company cars to do their jobs (e.g. sales reps), they are often provided to senior staff purely for status reasons. The practice of receiving company cars also varies between countries — for example in France they are uncommon. This is something for the Human Resource Planner to consider if s/he works for a pan-European or multinational organization. The message is perhaps that just as company cultures are reflected by the benefits given, so are national cultures.

Should cash be paid instead of benefits? It would certainly make administration easier and it could be argued that it is the most flexible system of all, as it allows employees to spend the money on what they wish.

PAUSE TO REFLECT

What social responsibilities might organizations have in this respect?

The people on the lowest incomes may not be able to afford the same level of benefits (e.g. pensions and life assurance cover) that can be provided by an employer. Since the employer basically buys these benefits in 'bulk', it means the cost is relatively low for the individual employee. Moreover, some of us need to be protected from ourselves! If we just received cash, perhaps we'd be tempted just to spend it all on life's luxuries rather than invest for our old age or emergencies. This concern is mirrored in the government's push to make it compulsory for all employees to have 'stakeholder' pensions.

Making benefits reinforce strategy. Benefits are part of the whole remuneration package and can be used to send out messages to employees about organizational expectations — such as stay with us for five years and you'll get an extra two days holiday, or reach a certain grade and receive a company car.

Communicating the value of benefits. It is unlikely that many employees realize the financial value of their overall benefits package, even though it could be worth up to 30% of their total remuneration. It is therefore in the organization's interest to regularly communicate this (primarily in retaining staff and for comparison with remuneration offered by competitors). This can be achieved by an annual statement to each employee, putting a financial value on each benefit.

Flexible benefits. These have commonly become known as '*Cafeteria*' benefits. We all have different aspirations and needs, which change throughout our working lives, and this system allows employees to pick and choose benefits from the 'menu' on offer by the employer. For example:

☛ Enhanced maternity pay (that is, more than the statutory minimum) or lengthy paternity leave is of no use to me if I don't have, or intend to have, children
☛ A season ticket loan is of no use if I walk to work
☛ And a company car is of no use if I don't drive.

Sounds great? A few years ago it seemed that this approach was going to really take off and become the standard way benefits were organized, but it never happened. The reason is that it is administratively complex (and legally complex on occasions). Firstly, how do you value the benefits in comparison to each other? Secondly, you'll probably need to employ more people (and computer software) to take care of the administration it generates, particularly if it's a large organization and people can make fresh choices over time.

07-7

(5)   The Medical Insurance 'Paradox'

Returning to the issue of social responsibility, private medical insurance is an interesting example of the benefits paradox, or put another way, 'when is a benefit not a benefit?'

Which sections of society need medical attention the most? The young and the old.

Which sections of society are least likely to be covered by private medical insurance? The young and the old.

This benefit primarily covers the healthiest age group in the population as a whole — so what is the 'benefit' to staff and what is the benefit to society?

ACTIVITY 14

Consider your own personal situation. What are your motivators and life priorities and how do these affect the benefits you would choose? Of all the benefits listed above (*except the car*), tick the five you would choose. In the space provided, state why you have chosen them.

☐	Pension	☐	Medical insurance
☐	Personal accident insurance	☐	Permanent health insurance
☐	Death in service benefits	☐	Relocation expenses
☐	Annual leave (although legislation now gives minimum levels)	☐	Enhanced maternity leave
☐	Payment of telephone bills	☐	Paternity leave
☐	Season ticket loans	☐	Payment of professional subscriptions
☐	Long-service awards	☐	Subsidized catering
☐	Subsidized mortgage	☐	Sports and social facilities
☐	Sabbatical leave	☐	Time off for public duties.

 ### 07-7-3   Current Approaches to Rewards

In the 1960s and 70s, the personnel management approach was purely directed at financial rewards. It did not recognize the strategic elements of rewards and failed to integrate pay with other personnel processes. Salary administrators were there to police the pay system, making sure that everyone stuck to rigidly defined procedures for grading jobs and salary progression. These people were only concerned with 'white collar' employees and line managers did what they were told. Manual workers' pay was left in the hands of industrial relations officers and work study staff.

These practices reflected how the organizations were managed and structured, with extended hierarchies and vertical communications systems. Progression up the hierarchy was mainly by regrading and often by means of fixed increments within grades or a 'pay spine' (as per our earlier incremental example).

The prevailing job evaluation systems were concerned with measuring *job size,* so that jobs could be placed in appropriate grades in the hierarchy. The evaluation schemes were often complex, rigid, paper-intensive and administratively unwieldy. They looked at internal relativities, and at jobs that were defined by lengthy job descriptions. *The systems focused on jobs, not people.*

Although market pressures were acknowledged, they were seen as something to be kept out of the system. As we noted under 'market subsidy', the pressures had to be bowed to on occasions, paying market premiums when necessary, but these were regarded very much as last resort measures. Benefits (which were referred to as 'fringe' benefits) started to become more common, but were often a means of tax avoidance rather than part of a rewards strategy (company cars really took off during government attempts to control inflation through incomes policies — that is, only allowing certain pay rises nationally).

The 1980s saw the abandonment of incremental systems in the private sector and performance-related pay (PRP) came into prominence. The traditional job evaluation schemes began to be seen as too rigid for the new flexible, de-layered organizations. *'Reward Management'* became a popular term at the end of the 1980s, de-emphasizing the role of money as the sole motivator and moving away from a status system.

Rosabeth Moss Kanter noted:

'Status, not contribution, has traditionally been the basis for numbers on employees' pay checks. Pay has reflected where jobs ranked in the corporate hierarchy — not what comes out of them'.

07-7

Armstrong and Murlis (1991) added:

'The essentially static techniques of "salary administration" have developed into the dynamic approach of reward management. The emphasis is first on performance, recognizing that the motivation to improve and the rewards for achievement must extend not only to the high-flyers, but to staff at all levels who help to achieve the success of the organization. Secondly, the emphasis is on flexibility. Reward management processes need no longer be confined to the straitjackets of rigid salary structures and elaborate job evaluation schemes'.

At the beginning of the 1990s the term *'New Pay'* came into being. This implied that the reward system had to reflect the organization's goals, values and cultures, together with the pressures emanating from a global economy. Lawler (1990) advocated *people-based* as opposed to *job-based* pay. That is, paying people for their value in the market and in recognition of their knowledge and skills.

Schuster and Zingheim (1992) stated the fundamental principles of 'new pay' as:

☞ Employees are the main reason the organization is able to remain competitive and to compete effectively. New pay is consistent with the organization becoming world class by forming a partnership with its employees.

☞ Management means leadership, not hierarchy and bureaucracy.

☞ Employee communications are critical to success. Pay is one key element of communication that can be managed so as to convey the right message about values, performance expectations and standards.

☞ Remuneration programmes should be designed to reward results and behaviour consistent with the key goals of the organization.

☞ Pay is above all an employee relations issue. Employees have the right to decide whether the values, culture and reward systems of the organization match their own.

☞ Remuneration should be regarded as an element of the organization's total management processes. Pay can be a positive force in organizational change.

☞ Basic, variable and indirect pay are elements of a remuneration strategy, not separate and independent.

☞ The main thrust of new pay is in introducing variable pay to employee groups where most organizations pay only basic pay.

☞ The emphasis is on team as well as individual rewards, and on partnership, such that employees share financially in the organization's success.

☞ The advantages of variable pay are seen as its ability to form partnerships between the employees and the organization, and to vary pay costs with performance, so as to create the need for high levels of teamwork, and to support quality and customer value goals.

☞ Organizations should determine the total remuneration mix and level of benefit costs they can sustain and then manage benefits so as to free money for spending on direct pay, particularly variable pay, where the return on the organization's investment is greater.

 ## 07-7-4 Prevailing Reward Structures

We've touched on a number of reward structures, but let's go through them a little more systematically. Armstrong and Murlis (1991) identify seven main types of reward structure:

☞ Graded structure
☞ Individual job range
☞ Progression related to competence
☞ Job families
☞ Spot rates
☞ Pay spine
☞ Rate for age.

(1) Graded structures

These consist of a number of pay ranges or grades, with minimum and maximum figures. The employee moves within the grade, or grades, depending on performance, experience and length of service. Jobs are given grades reflecting their *size,* with comparable jobs slotted into the same grade.

Grades can have the previously mentioned increments, or allow the flexibility to apply a salary figure within the overall range. The range can be as narrow or broad as the organization decides. The mid-point tends to be the 'rate for the job'. The size of grades will determine the amount of overlap between the maximum of one grade and the minimum of another.

 ACTIVITY 15

What implications do you think there are from having grades which overlap significantly? Note down your thoughts.

07-7

Now compare your answer with ours in Appendix 1.

Progression through length of service is now virtually nonexistent, with the emphasis being on performance. This enables the top performers to be advanced more quickly. The other advantages include ease of salary planning, because there are clear pay boundaries and progression steps, and a sense of fairness and transparency is promoted — but only if there is in place some analytical process to determine the relevant grade for each job.

Disadvantages include a level of inflexibility since it is not always easy to place unusual jobs into a grade, and the difficulty of rewarding particularly high-flying individuals. Such systems tend to be subject to 'drift' over time, as there is a tendency to gradually place jobs in higher grades, particularly if the job holders have been in place for a long period.

(2)   Individual job ranges

These result in the payment of salary ranges to each individual job, as opposed to comparable jobs being grouped together. They can be useful where jobs are changing rapidly, or when organizations have jobs that are very diverse. They can also easily reflect the external labour market without problems for internal differentials. The downsides include administrative problems and inconsistency, particularly as organizations grow.

(3)   Progression or pay curves

These are often used where it is difficult to analyse jobs in terms of their size. The work carried out by each employee may depend on their capabilities and experience — think perhaps of scientific staff. The market rate for individual jobs may also be a dominant factor. Here then, progression curves may be useful, where different pay rates are allocated to different levels of competence and the prevailing market rate for that job. It is normally the case that job holders will not move to a new pay level until they have reached a (previously agreed) level of competence.

An example of a pay curve is given below.

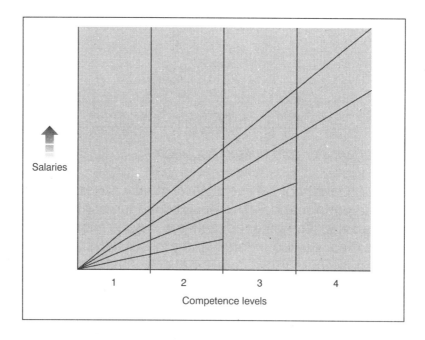

 **ACTIVITY 16**

What in your view are the advantages and disadvantages of having progression or pay curves? Note them here.

Advantages	Disadvantages

Compare your answers with ours in Appendix 1.

(4)   Job families

These can be used when an organization employs distinct groups of staff with different pay markets (we mentioned these in Section 07-3-4). For example, sales staff might be placed on a separate pay scale to those in IT. This allows varying practices for career progression to be put in place and allows the organization to follow pay trends in diverse markets.

Job families can also lead to feelings of unfair treatment if certain groups are lagging behind in the pay stakes. It is more difficult to maintain a consistent pay policy for the organization as a whole and market research will need to be kept up to date for each of the disparate groups.

07-7

'Broad-banded pay structures' are sometimes associated with job families. This is when existing grades or salary ranges are compressed into a smaller number of wide bands (typically four to five). An increasing number of fast-changing organizations are adopting this structure. Pay is managed more flexibly than in a traditional graded structure and more attention is paid to market relativities.

They have a number of aims, with two key ones being:

☞   To develop alternative methods of payment, mirroring a wider spectrum of employee development and contribution. This includes increased levels of competence, skill acquisition, continuous learning and flexibility.
☞   To facilitate horizontal career moves and internal mobility in flatter organizational structures through the provision of rewards for such moves. This promotes the message that advancement can take place through lateral as well as horizontal moves within the organization.

Broad-banding would look something like the diagram below, showing job families at IBM (from the CIPD's guide on broad banding, 1997).

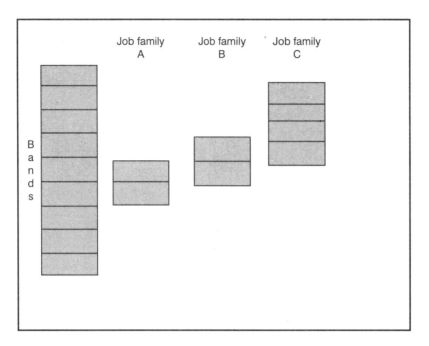

(5) Spot rates

These are used when there is only one pay rate for a specific job. Although it can be a point within a range, it is more likely to be just the one amount being the going rate.

The majority of manual workers have tended to be paid in this way. On the positive side, they do not create any expectations of salary progression, other than an annual 'cost of living' uplift. If everyone doing a job is on the same rate, there aren't any questions of favouritism or individuals being treated unfairly (whether the group as a whole feel they are underpaid is another matter). Also, a system of this kind allows the organization to respond quickly to changing circumstances. If, for example, a competitor a couple of miles down the road increases its pay rates, it can follow suit to prevent the mass exodus of its own staff. Finally, it makes administration very simple.

The disadvantages include lack of flexibility, as spot rates don't recognize increased knowledge and experience. This problem is exacerbated as the organization grows in size and complexity. They can be demotivating as there is no opportunity for progression and the assumption that there is a rate for the job is not always correct — particularly with administrative and professional roles.

(6) Pay spines

These are formed by a series of incremental points, ranging from the organization's smallest job to its largest. The spine will then normally be divided into grades, with automatic progression within the grade normally related to service. They have similar disadvantages to the grading system, but with the added problem that progression is not linked to performance. Although it may be possible to withhold an increment because of substandard performance, in reality this tends to be very rare.

(7) Rate for age

These systems also tend to be incremental and work on the basis that young employees will take time to become fully proficient in their roles. A standard example would be to pay them 75% of the full rate during their first six months of employment. On the plus side the administration is easy, but again they do not take into account performance. The employee may be 'up to speed' after three months, or may still be below the required efficiency threshold after nine.

07-7-5 Incentives and Bonuses

PAUSE TO REFLECT

What is the difference between a bonus and an incentive?

07-7

Incentives are meant to reward performance. Bonuses come in many forms and are not necessarily related to performance. Some organizations may award long service bonuses after, say, each five years of service (thus recognizing service, but not distorting the grading system, if one exists). The traditional Christmas bonus is a general thank you (or a general insult, depending on the size!).

Productivity payments have changed shape over the years and have been traditionally linked to manual and craft jobs. They used to have a scientific basis, with the individual components of each job task being measured and the time taken to complete them recorded. Standard times for each activity were then set, with bonuses being paid for meeting or exceeding targets. The emphasis today tends to be on negotiated flexibility agreements, which concentrate on methods of work, hours and other terms of employment.

Executive incentive schemes come in many forms. They aim to:

☛ Recognize the employee's contribution to the success of the organization
☛ Increase the employee's level of awareness of the organization's prime objectives and prompt them to concentrate on these
☛ Allow the employee to share in the organization's success
☛ Forge the link between remuneration and performance.

Some commentators say that if you need to pay incentive payments then you're hiring the wrong people. Well motivated people won't need a financial incentive, and if you are paying the right basic salaries, pay won't be an issue.

Perhaps, to some extent, incentive schemes are management controls — they say 'behave yourself and you'll be rewarded, but step out of line and you won't'. This is a view echoed by the management writer Kohn (1998), who stated:

'Rewards secure one thing — temporary compliance. When it comes to producing lasting change in attitudes and behaviour, however, rewards — like punishment — are strikingly ineffective'.

The view that pay is not a motivator is very common. But incentive schemes do recognize performance and contribution. They have some serious intrinsic problems however — if they are not administered fairly and consistently, and if the amounts paid fall from one year to the next they can be a *demotivator*.

Bonus or savings scheme?

Incentive schemes need to be reviewed on a regular basis to ensure they are achieving their objectives. Some may have been chugging along in the same form for so many years that no one can quite recall the original need for them, and maybe management doesn't have the courage to either amend or discard them. Often 95% of people know they are going to get an 'average' bonus — some know this right from the start of the year!

The philosophy is that if virtually everyone receives an average bonus then people are less likely to complain about discrepancies between themselves and their colleagues. In essence, if they know they'll be getting 5% at the end of the year, then it's no longer an incentive scheme — it's a savings scheme. Employees will use it to buy a new sofa or put it towards a holiday or whatever — but the point is *they will regard it as an entitlement — part of their basic pay — not something to strive for.*

When setting up an incentive scheme, several questions have to be addressed (perhaps in negotiation with trade union or staff representatives):

☞ How much pay is to be put at risk?
☞ What measures of performance will be used? These can be individual, including appraisal reports and target setting, or related to team or organization performance.
☞ What level of payments can be made?
☞ What is the frequency of payments to be?
☞ Which staff are to be included?
☞ What will be the link between incentive and remuneration?

Profit-sharing schemes

These come in two forms — 'approved' and 'non-approved'.

'Non-approved' schemes are traditional schemes that enable employees to share in a 'pool' of cash, using some sort of formula — perhaps by simply reaching a set level of pre-tax profit. The money tends to be allocated as a percentage of the individual's pay. In some companies the poorer performing employees do not receive a share.

07-7

'Approved' schemes were introduced by the government with the aim of allowing shares to be distributed to employees instead of cash. These had to be retained for a set number of years before being sold, free of tax. Although these were still known as 'profit-sharing', there was in fact no requirement for the company to make a profit in order to participate.

There are also the less well known *gain-sharing* schemes which allow employees to share in the financial gains made by the organization as a result of its improved performance. These can be based on, say, cost reduction or customer service.

PAUSE TO REFLECT

Can you think of another fundamental difference between gain-sharing and profit sharing? Consider how it is achieved.

Profit sharing is based on more than improved productivity. Certain factors outside the employees' control contribute to profit, such as changes in the economy or taxation. Gain-sharing is related specifically to performance and productivity improvements within the control of employees.

 ## 07-7-6   Performance Management

Over the past decade or so, organizations have reduced levels of hierarchy to be more flexible and cost-effective. The reduction in staff has meant that those who remain have had to perform more effectively. That is, effective performance means that output can be maintained with fewer numbers, or productivity increased. This is vital both for the long-term success of the organization (and in some cases success just means surviving) and the individual employee — since mediocre performance is no longer acceptable.

The assumption is that if individuals can satisfy their own needs by reaching their objectives and at the same time contribute to the attainment of the organization's objectives, they will be more highly motivated and achieve greater job satisfaction.

There are four main stages, showing the route to rewards:

(1)   Planning performance
(2)   Managing performance
(3)   Reviewing performance
(4)   Rewarding performance.

Rewarding performance is the part of the process which aims to give employees some kind of return for meeting their targets. This is more than just financial remuneration and includes praise, greater opportunities for training and development, and promotion. A key facet, then, is that recognition and praise are vital to employees, irrespective of whether monetary gains automatically follow.

The *performance management cycle* (from Hay Consultants, 1996) is shown to illustrate the process, below.

Training, career development etc.

We have covered the move from job evaluation *(measuring the job, not the person)* to a more person-centred approach. Pay levels in general are decided largely by economic factors, but for individuals the factors deciding their overall remuneration are much more complex.

Michael Armstrong (1996) has summarized them as follows:

07-7

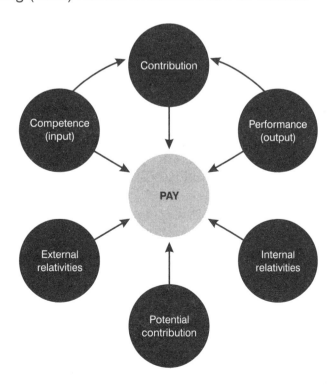

- *Inputs* made by individuals based on skills and competence that they can use effectively.
- *Outputs* of individuals resulting from them meeting targets or standards of performance.
- The *contribution* of individuals to achieving the purpose of the organization, their team or their role. This is measured by their results.
- *Internal relativities*. How the individual's job compares with others within the organization, in terms of factors such as knowledge and complexity.
- *External relativities* (market worth). What they are worth in the marketplace because of what they can do, or their expertise.
- *Potential*. Valuing individuals not just for what they can do now but what they can deliver in the longer term. (This is an important factor in the pay of some recent graduates.)

 ### 07-7-7   Measures to Retain Staff

The demand for talented staff is ever-increasing and so organizations must be both more focused and creative in their approaches to retaining talent. In his book *Futurewise*, Patrick Dixon (1998) has highlighted that organizations will need to be even more flexible and inventive in their outlook. Strong leadership will be necessary, promoting feelings of not only trust and belonging in the workforce, but also developing a greater cultural sensitivity in the face of globalization and technological advances. The 'talent management' strategy involves creating a winning environment by developing a high-achieving organization with values and brand images of which employees will be proud. This involves asking why people would want to join the organization and how the corporate culture, vision and values are likely to attract and retain the high performers. This is supported by competence in coaching, mentoring, regular feedback and sponsoring. Talented people need to be moved and promoted frequently, even during the formative stages of their careers. It may also be necessary to break existing remuneration policies to retain those with the greatest ability.

Longer-term developmental mentoring is vital, enabling people to talk in depth about their careers, work and aspirations. This approach is echoed by Eberhard Von Koerber, head of ABB Europe, who says:

> *'It's the soft investment that makes us competitive. It's about making use of brains that are 90 per cent under-used. People who don't understand this have no access to the solution of our poor competitiveness in Western Europe.'*

Coaching encompasses a number of activities that aim to bring out the best in people and cement their relationship with the organization.

The key features are:

☞ Active listening
☞ Questioning
☞ Giving praise and recognition
☞ Building rapport
☞ Creating trust
☞ Being non-judgemental
☞ Being candid and challenging
☞ Giving encouragement and support
☞ Focusing on future opportunities.

Staff retention may be affected by a range of factors, some or all of which will need to be considered and, when necessary, improved. These include:

☞ *Prospects.* Surveys into the factors that encourage employee loyalty nearly always put healthy career prospects ahead of high pay. The message to employees is that people will respond to the offer of a reliable and challenging position, within a visible scale of progression.

☞ *Recognition.* As mentioned above, the manager's appreciation for a job well done should be conveyed. As Blanchard and Johnson (1982) famously said in the *The One Minute Manager*, 'Help people reach their full potential – catch them doing something right'.

☞ *Pay and benefits.* Should be perceived by staff as fair if dissatisfaction in certain groups is not to arise. Similarly, if the organization does not pay as well as its competitors it will experience staff drift, particularly amongst the most talented.

☞ *Working conditions.* A poor environment, particularly in our increasingly health conscious times, will both hinder performance and increase dissatisfaction.

☞ *Working relationships.* Also affect the level of absenteeism and turnover.

☞ *Job design.* Jobs need to be designed to produce variety, opportunities for learning and growth, and provide a suitable 'fit' with the individuals doing them.

☞ *Commitment.* Managers must explain and champion the organization's aims to gain the commitment of staff. They must help the individual to recognize that their own contribution is worthwhile.

☞ *Performance.* If employees do not feel adequate in their jobs they are unlikely to stay for very long. They need to receive clear guidance on what is expected from them and the necessary training to achieve it.

☞ *Selection and promotion.* Appointing people who are not yet ready for the demands of a particular job is likely to lead to a swift drop in morale and to voluntary terminations.

☞ *Expectations.* Although a key part of staff management is motivation, if expectations are raised about progress or potential rewards which are not then met, there will be a subsequent drop in commitment.

☞ *Poor supervision or management.* In reality, this is an amalgamation of the above factors.

07-7

 **ACTIVITY 17**

How would you rate current procedures and practices in your organization in relation to these ten key retention factors? Which areas show most room for improvement?

Retention factors	Rating	Areas needing improvement
Prospects		
Recognition		
Pay and benefits		
Working conditions		
Working relationships		
Job design		
Commitment		
Performance		
Selection and promotion		
Expectations		
Poor supervision or management		

The line manager's role in HR planning and staff retention

There is not, or should not be, a chasm between the work of HR practitioners and line managers in the supervision of staff. It is critical to remember that line managers are in fact the personnel managers for their team. They are responsible for performance, for training and development, discipline, welfare, counselling, recruitment and termination. They are accountable for planning, controlling and organizing work, for motivating and for achieving results through people. The role of HR is to support line managers, not replace them or a chunk of their role. They should support line managers through the provision of services, such as training and development — essentially helping the manager to manage.

It has sometimes been thought that the HR function has taken over staff responsibilities from the line manager. However, recent moves towards employee empowerment and the delegation of authority to lower levels has helped to reverse this mindset. The position of line managers in this structure is shown on the diagram below.

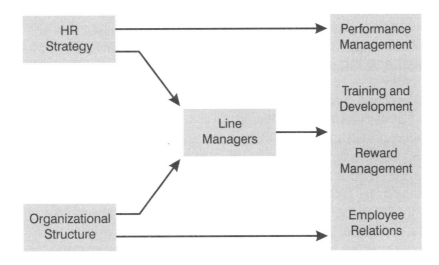

07-7

The line manager's responsibility for the training and development of staff is a particularly important one in today's climate of diversification and rapid product/system development. If organizations do not address this as a priority, giving it the resources it needs, a vicious circle can quickly develop. This has been prevalent in a number of call centres which tend to have relatively high turnover anyway, due to factors such as boredom and 'burnout'. The higher the turnover, the more new recruits are taken on. This means a greater volume of training, but less time and resources per capita, which in turn leads to more pressure on both new and existing staff, creating higher turnover and so the cycle begins again.

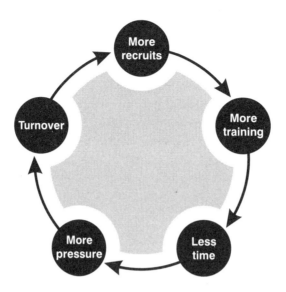

Preventive measures open to managers to stem turnover and increase job satisfaction include:

☞ *Work rotation* — allowing individuals to have a regular 'change of scene' within their organization or work unit, to both decrease the risk of boredom and increase their overall breadth of skills/knowledge.

☞ *Teamworking* — to engender overall commitment and motivation. The esprit de corps may be further enhanced if the teams are allowed a high degree of self-management.

☞ *Employee participation* — which can range from two-way team briefings and 360 degree appraisal to works councils and staff committees. Employees who feel their voice is heard and acted upon will be more enthusiastic (a 1999 study by PC manufacturer Toshiba of 150 businesses found that 68% believed that enthusiasm among the workforce was the single most important factor in increasing productivity).

☞ *Improved training in supervision* — so that best practice can be promoted and spread by those who are 'first in line'.

☞ *Improved communication* — from suggestion schemes and cascade briefings to intranets and email bulletin boards.

☞ *Improved developmental opportunities* — funding long-term qualification courses, for example, will help to tie employees to the organization for a number of years, particularly if payback clauses are included.

Each organization must, however, choose the methods and strategies applicable to its own culture, structure and values.

APPENDIX 1

COMMENTARY ON ACTIVITIES

Activity 1

Contracts *of* service are for people who work directly for one organization.

Contracts *for* services are for people 'outside' the organization, who provide services to it, normally on a temporary basis.

Activity 2

Your response will, of course, be unique to your organization. However, six fundamental objectives of Human Resource Planning are often identified:

(1) *Costing.* Forecasting future staff costs is a necessity for most organizations. Planning aids cost reduction by working out in advance how staffing might be accomplished most efficiently. It is vital when new projects or business ventures are being considered, in informing the decision-making process. Too high a workforce cost may mean a project does not go ahead.

(2) *Recruitment.* Human Resource Planning provides data on which recruiters base their activities. It indicates what gaps exist between the demand for and supply of people with specific skills. It is a basis for deciding who to recruit and by what methods (e.g. using a 'headhunter' instead of advertising). Planning aims to ensure that there are neither too many nor too few recruits to meet future operational needs.

(3) *Training and development.* Following on from the recruitment part of the process, Human Resource Planning aims to identify what skills training and development activity need to be arranged to ensure that the organization is *capable* of meeting its business objectives and that existing employees have the required skills and knowledge at the right time.

(4) *Collective bargaining.* When there is a strong trade union presence in an organization, Human Resource Planning provides vital information to be used in the bargaining process. If, for example, a long-term deal is being negotiated, data provided by its forecasts can be used to calculate how much extra pay to allow in return for greater productivity.

(5) *Redundancy/Redeployment.* In anticipating future redundancies or possible redeployment of staff, Human Resource Planning allows advance action to be taken. This may take the form of a freeze on recruitment, early retirements or retraining, with the aim of reducing the numbers involved. Cost savings through lower redundancy payments should then be achieved. Additionally, although redundancies may not

be avoided, there may be a less damaging impact on employee relations through early warning being given, as opposed to sudden announcements of redundancy.

(6) *Accommodation*. A practical benefit resulting from good planning can come from information relating to future needs for office/factory/warehouse space and car parking facilities. This concerns both situations of expansion and contraction. Once again, it has an impact on costs, helping to avoid sudden reactions to situations which could have been foreseen.

Activity 3

The two key determinants impacting on the quality of forecasting are:

(1) *Time period*. It is normally possible to look six to twelve months ahead without major difficulties. However, if the organization has to predict three, five or even ten years in advance, the chances of problems arising increase dramatically. But some businesses have to do this, especially if they are investing in major capital projects (e.g. oil exploration), or product research (e.g. pharmaceutical products, which can often take well over a decade to bring onto the market). Over the last 20 years the UK has witnessed some pretty violent swings in the demand for labour, with certain parts of the country and certain industries sometimes having severe problems in finding employees with the skills they require. This has sometimes meant a widening of their geographical labour pool, perhaps from national to international sourcing of staff.

(2) *Business sector*. The type of activities the organization is involved in is critical to the success of forecasting. A stable environment or business sector will make planning easier than one which is affected by market volatility. An example of the former might be a local authority which, save for a radical change in the political climate, is able to predict with relative certainty the resources it needs to efficiently provide the services entrusted to it by the electorate.

Activity 4

Although our list is not exhaustive, some of the main reasons are:

- To take up a job with another organization
- To retire
- To enter full-time education
- Promotion or demotion
- To become self-employed
- Relocation of partner to another job elsewhere in the country or abroad
- Illness
- Career break, perhaps to start a family
- Redundancy
- Dismissal

☞ End of a temporary contract
☞ Internal transfer.

Activity 5

(1) Research, as far as possible, the role of the department and the job.
(2) Prepare a list of questions and place them in a logical sequence.
(3) Choose an appropriate location for the interview — this should be quiet and free from distraction.
(4) You may also wish to visit the person's actual place of work, particularly if, for example, they are using machinery. This will also give a good idea of the working environment.
(5) Try to relax the interviewee, as they will often be anxious. The usual route is to engage them in small talk, offer them a tea or coffee and thank them for sparing their valuable time.
(6) Inform them that you are only after facts, not opinions.
(7) Clarify any general or vague answers with follow-up questions.
(8) Ensure the information you are given and note down is not judgemental.
(9) Ask *open-ended* questions which prompt people to describe their role.

Examples might be: *'Tell me about . . .',*
                        'Describe to me . . .'
                        'Give me some examples of . . .'

(10) Avoid *leading* questions, which might suggest what the answer should be.

Examples might be: *'Would you agree with that . . .?'*
                        'I'm sure that you must . . .?'
                        'It must be difficult to . . .?'

(11) Try to get specific examples of what the job holder actually does.
(12) Let them describe the limits of their authority.
(13) Tell them who else you'll be speaking to (supervisors and colleagues — this should help to counter any exaggerations).
(14) Take full notes — ask the post holder to slow down if necessary, so that you get all the information you need. It is possible to use a tape recorder, but this can be off-putting to some people.
(15) Clarify essential points with them by summarizing what they have said.
(16) Use closed questions when you only want short, factual answers.

Examples would be: *'How many . . .?'*
                        'How often . . .?'
                        'Who . . .?'
                        'When . . .?'

(17) When the interview is drawing to a close, ask them if there is anything they would like to add, or anything that has not been covered.
(18) Explain to them what the next stage in the process will be.

(19) Thank them for their time and help.
(20) Check and write up your notes *as soon as possible.* Straight away is best — it's amazing how quickly the memory fades, or how notes which seemed perfectly clear at the time now look like they've been written by a GP.
(21) Write the job description.
(22) Check the job description with the post holder and the relevant manager and get both to sign it off.

Activity 6

In most cases, redundancy occurs from a general reduction in business. However, it is perfectly possible for expanding businesses to make jobs redundant if certain *types* of work or skills are no longer required. Large organizations, following best practice and endeavouring to negate the bad publicity (both internal and external) which the dreaded 'R' word brings, will normally try to retrain or redeploy the people affected.

Activity 7

The answer is effective Human Resource Planning! If you can look ahead some months, or even years, to potential downturns in business, product changes or relocations, this should help in minimizing redundancies. Let's give an example of a pharmaceutical company. It may be manufacturing a drug which is protected under a patent. Let's say the patent lasts five years. The company knows that at the end of the fifth year, its competitors (who by this time will have geared-up to produce identikit products) will undercut its sales with cheaper, so called 'generic' drugs. So, unless it has other drugs in the pipeline, the company will know in advance that it may have to reduce its workforce. Perhaps as much as two years in advance, it may start taking appropriate measures — such as not replacing employees who retire or resign, or only taking on temporary staff during that period. In reality, it is planning the human side as it would do for its raw materials. During the last year or so, the company could also retrain employees in the production of new drugs.

Activity 8

Practical measures include:

☞ Allowing time off to look for jobs and attend interviews
☞ Allowing the use of company materials, such as paper, printers and photocopiers to produce CVs
☞ Secretarial help to type CVs
☞ Up-front references can be supplied to send with CVs
☞ Company cars can be used to attend interviews, or travel expenses provided
☞ Certain contractual clauses can be waived, such as those normally preventing employees joining competitors within a certain time period

- ☞ Managers and directors themselves can contact other organizations or counterparts to discuss potential opportunities
- ☞ A lump-sum payment may be granted to enable individuals to meet their own training needs.

Activity 9

Person A

- ☞ Right at the start, ask her what *she* would like during the next 3 months. That also, of course, applies to Frank and Siobhan.
- ☞ Arrange to take Susan to say an initial hello to her new workmates as soon as possible. This could involve having lunch with them.
- ☞ If they have after-work social activities, get her to participate.
- ☞ Let her spend, say, 30 to 60 minutes with her new supervisor, discussing how the team works and being given an overview of their products.
- ☞ Arrange specific product training — perhaps one day per week, leading up to the transfer.
- ☞ Allow her time to sit alongside some of her new colleagues, listening in to their calls.
- ☞ Show her to her new workstation. Allow her to make it her own by adding personal items (photos, etc.). Discuss any technical differences from her former equipment (her new stuff could be older or newer, better or worse).

Person B

- ☞ Frank will need to begin training as soon as possible — and on a full-time basis if he can be released from his last post five days per week.
- ☞ The training will be a combination of classroom-based (i.e. product knowledge, customer knowledge and sales techniques) and field-based (shadowing other sales people, being introduced to existing customers on his 'patch' and shown how best to plan his time).
- ☞ It is likely that, once trained, he would be on probation in his new job — that is, a trial period of perhaps three or six months. This is when both he and his boss decide if he is really cut out for the role. He will need plenty of 'hand-holding' during this time and regular appraisal sessions.
- ☞ A new contract of employment will need to be drawn up, containing the above in formal terms. He could still be made redundant in three to six months.

Person C

Siobhan's case takes us into a whole new arena. She should be fine with the job itself, but there are other considerations. Firstly, from her perspective, does she really want to move to another area? She may be very happy where she lives and may have a family. Perhaps her partner has a good job in the area. So part of the HR practitioner's role may be to 'sell' the new area to both her and her nearest and dearest.

This could be done by:

- Allowing her to try the new job and area for, say, three months. This could involve her staying in a hotel during the week and returning home for the weekends. The organization would bear all the associated costs.
- Paying for her family members to visit the new area.
- Using a headhunter to help her partner find a job in the new area.
- Registering them with a number of estate agents in the area to give them an idea of the property market.
- Providing information on schools in the new area.

Again, a new contract of employment will need to be constructed.

Activity 10

Although certainly not comprehensive, some of the resulting cost and management implications may be:

- An increase in overall advertising and advertising expenditure for this group of recruits. The organization may have to use bigger, brighter adverts. It may have to repeat them more regularly and advertise in a wider array of journals (as well as on the Internet). Bearing in mind that a full page colour advert in a leading IT journal will be in excess of £10,000, without any guarantee of success, costs could spiral rapidly.
- An increased use of agencies or headhunters. Some organizations may see this as a better bet, as in some cases they will only pay a fee when an appointment is actually made. However, even for relatively junior recruits this is unlikely to be less than 20% of the first year's remuneration. For more senior staff the going rate is 33%. Moreover, the fee is normally paid in three 'tranches': a third on taking the assignment, a third on presenting a shortlist, and the final third on appointment of the candidate. So for an applicant on a remuneration package of £80,000 this would come to £26,400.
- Increased spending on one section of the workforce may well have a distorting effect on other groups. For example, it may result in lower salaries or fewer staff in these 'less critical' areas. It may mean that less can be spent on advertising for other staff and possibly, for smaller organizations, less spending on product advertising.

Activity 11

Structured interviews do not always promote a relaxed atmosphere. This may, in turn, put candidates off from entering into an open two-way dialogue. These problems can be partly avoided by semi-structured and multiple approaches.

Activity 12

There are perhaps three considerations:

☞ Buying such tests can be very expensive.
☞ Recruiters using the tools need to be trained, which can sometimes be lengthy and add substantially to the overall cost.
☞ If too many organizations use the same tools, then candidates may come across the same ones in quick succession, with the risk of distorting the results. This would be particularly applicable to graduates and school leavers.

Activity 15

Overlapping grades or pay ranges have implications for the management of pay policy. The amount by which a high-performing employee can earn more than someone on a higher grade who is not as effective will depend on the organization's culture and how good its performance management processes are.

The culture question again relates to how transparent a system is. In some organizations, particularly if a purely market-driven *laissez-faire* approach is in operation (or where simple favouritism is allowed to flourish), employees are sometimes contractually obliged not to disclose their salaries because of the damage this might do to internal harmony and employee relations.

Activity 16

Advantages:

☞ Flexibility to reward individual performance
☞ Such a system recognizes that competence can increase both over time and through experience
☞ They can easily relate different pay markets to individual jobs
☞ They do not rely on measuring or evaluating the job.

Disadvantages:

☞ Comparing jobs is difficult
☞ Equal pay for equal value comparisons are difficult due to the lack of analytical job measurement (which could ultimately mean a legal challenge)
☞ They could, consequently, be demotivational if any staff members feel they are being treated unfairly.

APPENDIX 2

USEFUL RESOURCES

Other (linked) Universal Manager dossiers:
     Dossier 12:   *Managing for High Performance*
     Dossier 13:   *Managing Harmoniously*

Specialist Journals
The two leading generalist HR journals currently in the UK are *People Management* (published by the Chartered Institute of Personnel and Development) and *Personnel Today* (published by Reed Business Information Ltd).

Publications
K Abosh (1998), 'Variable Pay: Do We Have the Basics in Place?', *Compensation and Benefits Review*, May/June.
ACAS (1994), *Introduction to Payment Systems*, ACAS, London.
K Adams (1998), 'Re-thinking Competency-based Pay', *Competency*, Autumn.
N Anderson & V Shackleton (1993), *Successful Selection Interviewing*, Blackwell, Oxford.
N Anderson & V Shackleton (1994), 'Informed Choices', *Personnel Today*, November.
M Armstrong (1996), *Employee Reward*, CIPD, London.
M Armstrong & H Murlis (1991), *Reward Management: A Handbook of Remuneration Strategy and Practice*, Kogan Page, London.
K Blanchard and S Johnson (1982), *The One Minute Manager*, Hazel Watson & Viney, Aylesbury.
J Bramham (1994), *Human Resource Planning*, CIPD, London.
J Bridgford & J Stirling (1994), *Employee Relations in Europe*, Blackwell, Oxford.
CBI/Hay Management Consultants (1996), *Trends in Pay and Benefits Systems*, CBI, London.
CIPD (1997), *CIPD Key Facts — Recruitment*, (Summary of the IPD Recruitment Guide 1996), CIPD, London.
D Cooper & I Robertson (1995), *The Psychology of Personnel Selection*, Routledge, London.
I Deutsch (1997), *The Survivor Syndrome*, ECW Press.
P Dixon (1998), *Futurewise*, HarperCollins, London.
Equal Opportunities Commission (1997), *Code of Practice on Equal Pay*, London.
S Fine & M Getkate (1995), *Benchmark Tasks for Job Analysis*, Lawrence Erlbaum, New Jersey.
A Fowler (1993), *Redundancy*, CIPD, London.

D Guest & N Conway (1997), *Employee Motivation and the Psychological Contract*, CIPD, London.

N Gupta & J Shaw (1998), 'Financial Incentives are Effective!', *Compensations and Benefits Review*, March/April.

C Handy (1994), *The Empty Raincoat: Making Sense of the Future*, Hutchinson, London.

F Herzberg (1966), *Work and the Nature of Man*, World Publishing, Cleveland.

IES Report 386, *HR shared services and the realignment of HR*, Grantham Book Services.

Incomes Data Services (1995), 'Executive Benefits', *Management Pay Review*, No. 174.

T Keenan (2000), 'Fit for the job', *People Management.*

A Kohn (1998), 'Challenging Behaviorist Dogma: Myths about Money and Motivation', *Compensation and Benefits Review*, March/April.

E Lawler (1995), 'The New Pay: a Strategic Approach', *Compensation and Benefits Review*, July/August.

T Leap and M Crino (1993), *Personnel/Human Resource Management*, MacMillan.

C Legere (1985), 'Occupational Analysis' in *Human Resources Management and Development Handbook* (W R Tracey, ed.), AMACOM, New York.

P Lewis (1993), *The Successful Management of Redundancy*, Blackwell, Oxford.

G McBeath (1992), *The Handbook of Human Resource Planning — Practical.*

E McCormick, P Jeanneret & R Meacham (1972), 'A Study of Job Characteristics and Job Dimensions Based on the Position Analysis Questionnaire', *Journal of Applied Psychology*, vol. 56.

M Marchington & A Wilkinson (1996), *Core Personnel and Development*, CIPD, London.

A Maslow (1953), *Motivation and Personality*, Harper and Row, New York.

H Mintzberg (1994), *The Rise and Fall of Strategic Planning*, Prentice Hall, New York.

F Neale (1991), *Handbook of Performance Management*, CIPD, London.

Pearn Kandola (2000), 'Fit for the job', *People Management.*

D Pritchard & H Murlis (1992), *Jobs, Roles and People*, Nicholas Brealey Publishing, London.

S Rothwell (1995), *Human Resource Planning*, Routledge, London.

J Schuster & P Zingheim (1992), *The New Pay*, Lexington Books, New York.

E Suter (2000), *The Employment Law Checklist*, CIPD, London.

A Swift (2000), 'Beat the Clock', *The Guardian.*

R Taylor (2000), 'Beat the Clock', *The Guardian.*

J Toplis, V Dulewicz & C Fletcher (1997), *Psychological Testing: A Manager's Guide*, CIPD, London.

D Torrington & L Hall (1995), *Personnel Management: HRM in Action*, Prentice Hall, London.

Trends in HR Outsourcing can be obtained by contacting Philip Vernon on 020 7802 3709.

D Ulrich, M Losey & G Lake (1997), *Tomorrow's HR Management*, John Wiley, New York.

H Vandevelde (2000), *Harnessing Technology for Career Success*, Trotman, London.

A Vowles (2000), 'Screen test', *People Management.*

B Williams (2000), 'Beat the Clock', *The Guardian.*

M Williams (2000), *The War for Talent: Getting the Best From the Best*, CIPD, London.

C Woodruffe (1993), *Assessment Centres: Identifying & Developing Competence*, CIPD, London.

USEFUL WEB SITES

Should you find that any of the links below is not working, check with the Universal Manager site (www.universal-manager.com) where links are updated frequently.

Example job boards:

www.stepstone.co.uk
www.topjobs.co.uk
www.monster.co.uk
www.reed.co.uk
www.select.co.uk
www.stepstone.com
www.doublecuff.com
www.OneClickHR.com
jobs.guardian.co.uk

Flexible working:

www.new-ways.co.uk
www.fatherhoodproject.org
www.familiesandwork.org

Further resources:
www.universal-manager.com

 **INDEX**

A
Ability tests 75, 79
ACAS 124
Alljobs 70
American Psychological Society 76
Andersen Consulting 20
Anderson 77
Annual appraisals 17
Application forms 72
Application service providers 22
Armstrong 42
Armstrong, Michael 111
ASDA 70
AskHR 21
Assessment centres 75, 84, 85, 90
Association of Graduate Recruiters 69
Atkinson, John 11

B
Biodata 75, 82
Blanchard & Johnson 113, 124
Bramham, John 14, 124
British Psychological Society 81
British Standards 26

C
Career plans 17
Case studies 13, 19, 21, 30, 64, 70, 73, 77
Chartered Institute of Personnel & Development 14, 66, 69, 81, 106, 124
Cisco 70
Classic trio 74
Cohort analysis 29
Competence-based recruitment 86, 89
Cook, Mark 73
Cooper & Robinson 82, 124
Core workers 11
Cranfield School of Management 21
Crino 26
Critical incident technique 39

D
Deutsch, Leon 64, 124
Developmental passports 17
Disability Discrimination Act 1995 61
Discrimination 61, 83, 84
Dixon, Patrick 112, 124
Down-shifting 60

E
Employment Protection (Consolidation) Act 1978 49
e-peopleserve 20
Equal Opportunities Commission 89, 124
Equal pay 94, 95

F
Five-fold grading system 43
Fowler, A 50, 124
Fraser, Munro 43
Fundamental Attribution Error 76
Futurewise 112, 124

G
Graphology 75
Greater Manchester Police 88, 89

H
Halo effect 75, 77
Hawthorne effect 40
Hay Management Consultants 46, 111
Headhunters 122
Hierarchical task analysis 39
Human resource planning – definitions 14

I
IBM 21, 106
ICL 70
Institute for Employment Studies 20
Internal promotion analysis 29
IPD 18

J
Job descriptions 41 – 43
Job family modelling 46

K
Kanter, R M 101
Keenan, Tony 86
Keynes, J M 27
Kohn, A 108, 125

L
Leap 26
Legere, C L J 34
Local labour markets 30

M
Management Charter Initiative 86
McBer behavioural competences 86
Medical examinations 73
Medical Reports Act 1998 73
Moloney, Karen 87, 88
MSL/McBer competence cluster 44

N
National Insurance 51
Nicholson, Tim 69

O

OneClickHR.com 22, 126
Online recruitment 69, 70
Outsourcing 12, 19, 20, 21, 51

P

Pearn Kandola 86, 87
Pensions 52, 97
People Management 124
Performance management 110 – 112
Peripheral workers 11
Person specifications 43
Personnel Today 124
PIR 89
Position analysis 37
Price Jamieson 76
Productivity trends 26
Profit sharing 109
Psychological contracts 17
Psychometric testing 22, 75, 81

R

Recruitment and Employment Federation 69
References 72
Repertory grid 39
Resource centres 59
Resource-based provision 27
Retirement 48, 52
Robertson & Makin 76
Rodger, Alec 43
Rothwell, S 17, 125

S

Seven-point plan 43
Shackleton 77
Shared services 20
Shell International 13
Skills planning 17
SMEs 26
Sourceuk.com 70
Spot rates 95, 106
Stability analysis 29
Staff turnover 28
Succession planning 17
Survivor syndrome 64

T

Taylor, Ros 76
The One Minute Manager 113, 124
Time series analysis 25
Toshiba 116
Toyota 30, 73
Treaty of Rome 95

V

Vandevelde, Helen 71, 126
Voluntary redundancy 53

W

Western Electric Company 40
William H Mercer Consultancy 21
Work study 25, 26